Towards Inner Freedom

Towards Inner Freedom

Society for the Inner Development of Man

Published by the Society for the Inner Development of Man
SIDM, PO Box 101, King's Lynn, Norfolk PE32 2FD, UK.

E-mail: sidm@sidm.freeserve.co.uk

First published 1999

ISBN 0-9535299-0-8

A CIP catalogue record for this book
is available from the British Library

Typeset by Agora, Robertsbridge, TN32 5EH
Printed in the UK by Antony Rowe Ltd, Chippenham, Wilts.

Contents

Jesus said:
If those who guide your Being say to you
"Behold the Kingdom is in the heaven,"
then the birds of the sky will precede you
if they say to you: "It is in the sea,"
then the fish will precede you.
But the Kingdom is in your centre
and is about you.
When you Know your Selves
then you will be Known,
and you will be aware that you are
the sons of the Living Father.
But if you do not Know yourselves
then you are in poverty,
and you are the poverty.

Introduction

There is considerable information on the Internet about both G. I. Gurdjieff and his pupil P. D. Ouspensky and it is obviously an advantage for this to be available. However it would appear that this consists of a limited and frequently repeated few facts extracted from popular books about the 'Work'. This gives the impression that it is a facile modern teaching, easily practised. This may do harm in that it may turn away those genuinely seeking knowledge because the correct start on a possible inner evolution may not be made.

The 'Work', a very old term, is an ancient practical method of work on oneself, brought to the West by Gurdjieff. It is not an invented teaching; it is knowledge from the past, gathered over many years and with considerable hardship by Gurdjieff, and recast into a psychological teaching suitable for the West and the present time. Serious students will find echoes of it at the core of all real religions. Gurdjieff said it was esoteric Christianity.

Books can acquaint one with the knowledge and arouse interest, but more is needed to progress. The 'Work' is taught orally, face to face, with students who feel deeply the need for knowledge not available from the outer fringes of established religions. The teaching takes place in small groups and the teacher is one whose understanding has grown through many years of working with an established 'school'. Groups are generally made up of people from very different backgrounds and are not a 'club' in the normal sense. The difficulties this presents is an essential part of the formation of a living entity that the groups can become, because the participants have to put aside their natural differences in their quest for inner freedom.

This book brings together extracts from 25 years of notes taken from meetings and Workdays in one such group based in Norfolk, England. This group has regular meetings, monthly meals, Workdays and fortnightly movements sessions. The meetings are an opportunity for the group to make observations which are individually answered by the teacher. Meals are a time for more informal discussion of ideas, and Workdays provide a chance for self-observation while trying to carry out internal exercises and practically working together as a group. Similarly, movements provide an opportunity to bring together and observe the head, the feelings and the body in a set of movements devised by Gurdjieff and set to his music.

The presentation of the ideas and exercises by the teacher and the observations of the students in this book gives an opportunity to experience the 'Work' in action and will no doubt provoke questions to which there is no immediate answer and thus an incentive for further study.

The Teaching

L. Something I have been thinking about is the amount of effort and energy that has been put into us. I don't know how others feel about it but I've been given a lot. There is some responsibility that comes with that. I feel that I have to start to do the Work, it's a new stage as opposed to dreaming about it. What do I take? I think I've been given a lot of goodwill recently, I have felt and experienced it I think. Whether that is imagination or not, I'm not sure.

I think being introduced to the Work has given me a very different way of looking at life, how to live life. It is a struggle to live that way and I am a long way from it yet. I feel a great deal of gratitude to you and everybody here for things that I can appreciate and for those I don't understand yet. I can't define it but I feel that it is something quite remarkable.

Because you're going away for a while you'll find it difficult. It is difficult here in a group and it is more difficult alone. You have to learn to take care of each other, try to keep it simple. To put it in simple terms, there is the possibility of growing something in us but we are faced with life which is an actual force. It is a force which in its own right feels that it has a claim to every bit of your energy. It wraps you up in a skin of imagination. If you can remember that, the purpose of your work is to become more aware and to grow and to feed what is inside you. The more you do that the more you will discover what it is that is stopping you. You will, if you carry on, become overwhelmed by it at some stage when you see what really lives your life is your arrogance, your imagination and your complete lack of anything to hang on to that is real. That is when you will need each other's help, and you can get help from here then, don't forget that. If you can go through that you can then really begin to work. It is the only thing worth having. One has to try to open up inside oneself. The understanding of why you want to come, why you want to work, you see. Once it gets sown inside you it will never stop. You may turn your back on it occasionally but it will never stop once it really has taken root and there will be two of you anyway to remind each other to work. And you won't be separated from here. You'll be surprised what can happen over a distance—if you wish it to happen.

J. I have been thinking that I am in debt, that I have received far more than I have put the effort in to get back. My effort has been so minimal and so infrequent and what I have got back has been so great. I did not think it was possible to be in debt in this Work, I thought one had to pay for what one received, so why do I feel like that?

It's true that you will be in debt, but it doesn't stop you trying to pay of course. This is the responsibility that has been mentioned. You are in debt to everybody before you through the centuries who has tried to get towards consciousness. One is in debt to all the teachers of the past who have tried to give us something.

When you make a start like this you see that you are not going to be enlightened overnight or even over a month or a year but you've got to make a start and then you get the idea of 'Can I do this?', 'Can I work on this?' Then, as I say, you become what is called a *working individual*, the Work has importance for you. You can't be aware of yourself all day long, you can't remember yourself for long but it's the actual process of beginning, the actual process of trying. The process of trying is in itself something quite separate. Someone who doesn't try, someone who is completely passive doesn't even know that there's any other alternative. If there is someone who knows or has an inkling that something can change, that there is something different, then from time to time they actually wish to be different; there's a beginning of a process, and seeing that they actually try to do something about it, instead of just being absolutely negative. They will for a moment say 'I will do this'; it may last for a minute or a couple of seconds but there is then at that moment a completely different individual. In the scale of differences of human beings that can be from a cabbage to someone who is really very highly enlightened. It's the beginning of the process that makes the difference. You start calling on a different level of energy. But we tend to do this and we just forget what we are trying to do, we don't see the importance of what we are trying to do, we don't really understand that we have this enormous possibility of being different. But it isn't all blazing lights; there is a difference you don't really understand, you become a different texture inside at certain times, something is growing inside and that difference in texture can absorb something different rather than the reactions that one gets all the time. Do you understand what I mean? Try to think about this as it is really very important. Unless you can really begin to think about this you can't move on.

Sometimes one notices in books, one reads about teachers, that at the end of their lives they invariably seem to say they changed their minds or went back to the beginning and I can absolutely understand what they mean, because one has a completely different idea of the whole situation. You have no idea what the Work is in the beginning, not the slightest idea. It is something quite different, but the idea of knowledge, the idea that there is knowledge and the form it can take is something quite different from what you imagine to begin with.

There is a danger of staying in one place too long; the essence of this Work is that it has been going on for thousands of years and it never appears to be constant, because it is always moving, always disappearing and then reappearing. You can't make statues or idols out of teachers, you can't idolize them and the Work itself sometimes has to be stirred up.

M. Do you think that there is a time when you are younger so to speak, that groups help you, then as you get older you are actually sacrificing something to spend that amount of time on groups? I have a feeling sometimes that if a person were very highly developed really all they would want would be just to be able 'to be' and they wouldn't really need anything else.

You see what this process, what we call life, does to us, it fragments everything. We can't keep two things together but if you could really feel *wish* you see, it would overcome a lot of that. I feel that to grow to be an individual capable of using one's own reason and looking after one's self, we take a risk. I take the risk with you certainly not understanding what I am trying to do at times and you floundering without any particular guidance. You have to learn to take chances, learn to try to reason, learn to open yourself to understanding. Try to think in a way that is not the normal way of thinking. In other words look for reality. And above all try to see that life as it is, is not reality for us. It's what the Sufis call the veil. The veil which covers. Before one really takes chances, take steps, try to see differently, try to accept that your situation is such that unless you do something there's no future. When you reach a certain level of understanding there comes a time when you wish to be with those with whom you have journeyed so far. There is a common understanding and a wish to serve and help.

One day outside my tutor's office I saw a small advertisement stuck on a board reading 'The proper study of mankind is man himself' and it gave the address of the Society for the Inner Development of Man. Without doubt, while reading this, I was struck by it and knew that it was something I had to follow up. I sent a letter, got a reply and I met someone from the group in Norwich.

To begin with, meetings were very hard, I didn't know why I was there nor did I want to be there.

It would be wrong to discard as nonsense the so-called 'strange events' which took me to Norfolk; in fact I find it remarkable.

Remembering Oneself

To remember yourself to begin with is to remember the body in which you are encased. You have to realise that there is a part of you which does not remember your body, a part which can float off in imagination and be in a state of dreaming. That is in a sense denial of the fact that you live in a particular body. So to remember yourself is to accept the fact that you live in this body. With your attention you become aware of the whole of it, and where you are and the situation you are in. You are aware of your feelings, thoughts, sensations, and as you practice this you become a completely different thing, the processes of energy inside you are different from when you are not like that.

There is a multiplicity of I's within us, and at each moment we belong to first one, then another. You might say the first object in looking at ourselves and seeing these different I's is to become stable, at least to begin with, and the observation of our centres—the emotional centre, the head and the motor centre—is an essential part. We have to really see to what extent we are unbalanced in that direction and learn to experience, to see what it would be to use emotion properly instead of letting it fly off with all this activity. Try to experience what it would be like to *think* rather than the same process just happening in the head. The danger is that emotional energies are so fast. It all comes back again to this same business, that we must start really and truly to see our situation.

Observation of oneself is normally something that goes on and off during the day. You may see yourself dreaming or you may see your inner talking or you may see some particular thing you do. To observe in quite a different way you have to be completely aware of yourself to begin with, your attention has to be focused, directed, on your body, to be aware of the fact that you are there in your body, that you are not in Hong Kong or somewhere else. I am here—'I', that is the first requirement. I use my attention and I direct my attention into my body. I get sensation in my body, at least I know I am in my body. Then an observation can possibly take place. Otherwise it is an observation of one part of oneself with another part of oneself, neither of which is really real.

To remember oneself is really a miracle in the definition of what a miracle is, that is the influence of a higher level on a lower level. When one really remembers oneself one sets in process a chain of events which creates different energies, as we see in the food octave.

I am sitting here now, I am aware of the sensation of my body sitting here. I am looking at that carpet and I remember, I try to understand why I wish to do this. It requires my attention. My attention is first of all on me then on the carpet, and it is then divided into two. Then it is divided into three by my understanding of what I am trying to do.

That is self-remembering. You needn't wait two years, you can do it tomorrow. It will appear to change because the act of doing it is changing you; it changes your inner being.

You see, if one can remember oneself, one's level is higher. If one really remembers oneself then one is really connected with one's real life which is up there, so to speak. You then touch your life. You can find that every time you really remember yourself you are touching something which has happened before and which has also happened in the future. It is your real life which exists complete from beginning to end.

The Inner and Outer Self

We are told that there is something inside us which comes from a level very much higher than we are. That the object of our being here is to allow that something to get experience, to enable it to grow. Perhaps occasionally we can accept this idea. It's very hard to do so though because we are not ordinarily in the place where such an idea can be accepted. There will be times when we can just accept this idea without any effort. Of course, if we are not in a place where we can accept an idea from a higher level, then this is unlikely.

That is why we have to learn to relax, drop all the rubbish we carry around with us and keep things clean. We have within us a higher level working all the time. It belongs there, but we don't make contact with it. If I can, by working, by relaxing, gather enough energy, I make contact with it. I then get a completely different view of things. I am on a higher level and have a different level of energy.

You can see that this inner part is completely enclosed in this outer level, which is so busy, so active all the time. If I can learn to quieten it, so that I can get rid of the opinions and attitudes which keep me closed up, then that inner part can be receptive and has the possibility of receiving something which is usually barred by our negativity and by our continuous activity. *Activity is not action.* Action is something quite different. It is quiet, it is clear, it is firm, because it understands what it has to do. Activity is a kind of thrashing around all the time, thinking one is going somewhere.

The outer part of us reacts to everything around it. We know that the force of life is incredibly strong.

Effort can be an enormous physical effort but, without understanding, it may be little more than slavery. Effort can also be an intense inner movement with wish, with intent. For example, I resolve to just maintain my presence from here to the bottom of the stairs and find this is almost impossible. Effort like that has to be renewed all the time. Once one gets the taste of that kind of effort, one can see how it can be applied in almost any direction in life.

Try to keep that effort. Each time it may be a tiny little step, but it's the depth of it that matters. And always try to bring in 'why?' Keep the understanding of why I have to do this because this is the difference. This is the third force, the third force that causes creation. This is the understanding which I must try to maintain all the time, and which makes the difference in all I do. Effort with understanding means I create something inside myself.

There is a thin film that covers the Earth, which is organic life. Each one of us is a tiny little cell in that film. It rules everything that you can see or feel on Earth. The outer part of you, the body with all its feelings, thoughts, and activity is also part of that life. So, it is reacting all the time to something in which it exists and to which it belongs.

The inner part of yourself is separate from that, can be separate and has a right to be separate. It has a right to grow. This is your task. You have to see that life is like that. The more you understand this situation, the more you will be able to struggle against it. Just to struggle against it blindly is useless.

In times past this outer life has been called the devil, it has been called all kinds of things because it was thought to stop people getting to God. But see it as a level of interacting energies, an 'Octave', which has every right to exist. Otherwise we wouldn't exist, nothing on Earth would exist. The Earth wouldn't be receiving energy which it receives from the Sun and beyond, and which is transformed into energy for life on the Earth.

We feel we have been given the possibility of moving out of that and up to the next level, a level that our inner part belongs to. Nothing else on Earth has been given that possibility. This is why if any being of a higher level wishes to get to a further level, it has to come down here first and go through this level of life. That is the only possibility of growth. That is why Christ and other particular individuals in the past, came. You might wonder why they came down here to suffer all this if they are capable of such inner growth. It is part of the process. It is this process that we have to try to understand if we are to make use of it.

You have to see that you are dual. Really see and try to understand this. See how action from the inner part of oneself is quite different from action from the outer part of oneself. How do you get action from the inner part of oneself? That's the question.

The answer really is, I think, when you cease to act purely reactively from the outer part of oneself. This comes from objective observation. When you see more and more the thing in which you are actually living, you begin to understand the situation. Without understanding you can work until you are blue in the face but it won't make a bit of difference. You have to understand what your situation is.

Objective self-observation, really truly objective self-observation is the beginning of that understanding. You see the situation over and over again. As we know, it's not very pleasant to begin to see that you are utterly, absolutely mechanical, that you consist of nothing more than habitual reactions. That you belong to an utterly, absolutely mechanical process which doesn't give a damn where you go. Its only concern is to milk you like a cow of your energy, which it uses and needs. Life doesn't want you to do anything other than be a complete slave to it. It wants you to remain there and forget everything else. You forget you are going to end up in a coffin, just as dust, with no possible future.

Remember the story of the man walking along the precipice on a little narrow path, which gets narrower and narrower until he can go no further. He tries to turn around only to find a bear walking up behind him. Then he sees, just out of reach, a rope. *Just that jump.* It's making that jump you see. Leaving behind all that's familiar in your thought, feelings and attitudes. If you can lose your attitudes and opinions then you are utterly and absolutely free. You get to the point where you can turn around inside yourself.

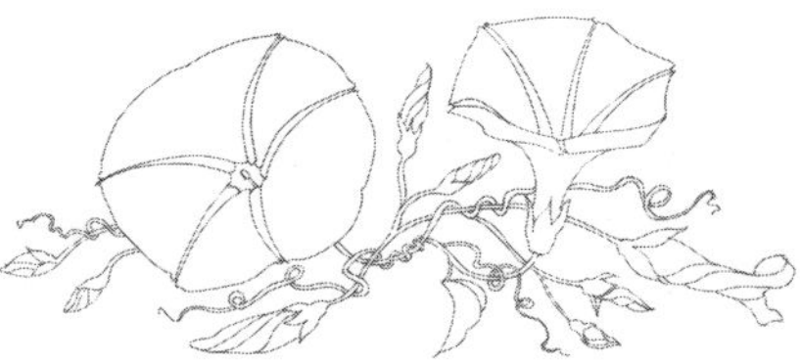

In 1983 I had my fourth child. I had four healthy children, a pleasant home, a good husband, but in the months and years that followed I was aware of a sense of something not being right. I felt 'the weight of the world'. I was not depressed but ill-at-ease. I joined groups such as a women's CND. I began to feel that I could do nothing and that it would have to be up to my children to do anything that could be done, whatever it was!

But I did know that I had to make contact with an old friend from school. It took a few years to make that phone call and one of the first things I asked about was what this group did that he belonged to. Did he have to wear hair shirts and open-toed sandals! It was suggested that I read 'In Search of the Miraculous'. This book amazed me, to think that this knowledge was sitting there in the library. I had walked by it and had to be pointed in the right direction. It still amazes me.

I was invited to a Workday. I was forty years old.

The Food Octave

Remembering oneself is the most important aspect of this Work because it sets into train the various processes which work inside us, that together we call the Food Octave. This is the means by which the ordinary energy we have is transformed into a much finer energy. It is this energy we have to learn to increase. Once one learns how, then it's something one has to do for the rest of one's life. You can accept that as you eat ordinary food it will be transformed into a different substance from which your body can take nourishment. It has to go through a process before it can be accepted as nourishment by your body. Your body has a means of doing that, providing that it is a food which is acceptable to human beings. Substances within our bodies act upon this ordinary food to change it into material acceptable to various organs, which demand finer and finer energies as the process progresses.

At a certain point this initial process—working with ordinary food—stops, and requires an additional impetus which comes from the air we breathe. As our bodies ingest our first food, so air also comes in automatically. It is beyond our control, if we stop taking it in we die very quickly. We can accept this idea of air being our second food quite readily. It may require more understanding to appreciate that impressions pouring in, in a continuous stream through our senses, are the third level of food and without which we cannot stay alive.

All of these foods are digested to a greater or lesser extent and the unused balance eliminated. We have very little choice about this process, which is Nature's way of keeping us alive, to provide her with energy. We can live to the end of our lives without ever once thinking about this.

However, as far as we can see, we are in the unique position on Earth in that we have the possibility of taking this process further, to help serve a different purpose. Each of the three foods entering the organism starts a train of increasingly fine energies we know as octaves. These are interdependent, but do not reach a conclusion, as they require a particular kind of shock to make them go further, when they can then provide a source of very fine energy. This shock—a conscious shock—requires the use of my attention, to remember myself. It works on the food of impressions. To be aware of oneself and aware of incoming impressions, at the time they are received, means that the food process is continued in a most remarkable way. This is what was called alchemy in the past.

When you try to remember yourselves, when you try to be quiet, be aware of the air coming in through your nostrils into your head, into your lungs. Nothing forced, just awareness of air entering your body. Allow it to remain there for just a few seconds and allow it to go out under control.

Try to understand, think about what air is. We take it in and we breathe it out, some of the oxygen remains in us and feeds us. We breathe out carbon dioxide. Trees breathe in carbon dioxide and breathe out oxygen. Air contains much more than that. It contains many substances and if we can really breathe consciously with an awareness of '*I am here*', at this moment, then I can take from the air food for the spiritual side of me from the many other substances it contains.

Aim

By some means or another I have got the idea that I really would like to live in a different way from how I live now. So I begin and then, after a while, I see that it is almost impossible to even consider achieving this. Yet there are moments when I can touch something different. I see I have the potential, and that is a little miracle. I discover that despite being the mechanical man I am, I have the possibility of not being like that, that's a fact. I am in some way composed of something here, and inside that, there seems to be something else. I'm finding out facts all the time, this is my situation.

You realise that you have very little attention, but if you think about it, you'll see the necessity of using what attention you have to try to relax, to try to work. You may not realise it at the time, but each little effort makes a difference. There is the possibility, the potential of being different inside, yet this has to grow slowly because once it grows it is permanent. It's not something that just withers away. When your understanding grows it is yours forever.

This way is called 'the way of the cunning man.' You know that if you were to start talking openly about the way one thinks, you would be considered a fool. This is where the question of aim comes in. I wish to succeed in living a life that feeds my inner life, but I have to accept the outer life and have to actually go into it, perform what I have to do. So I do it as well as possible, to make life easier for myself and not make myself obvious to other people. The cunning man learns to play the game, he has an aim beyond his day to day existence.

There is a value placed by society on our activities, and we have to manifest in this outer part of ourselves, to meet their values. If in fact the values of outer life were on a different level altogether, you could manifest from the inner part of you. This is society's problem at this time, the Third Octave is of more value than the Second Octave. We happen to exist in the Third Octave so we have to learn to cope with that, and for our own protection, we must find a way of living in it.

So I see that I am consumed by the need to succeed, this comes from the outer part of myself. It is important to succeed in quite a different way inside. There are people who lead a completely clockwork life very successfully, make lots of money, do lots of things, and they are following a line that they have followed many times before. There are others who have the courage to do things other people have never done; this depends on their being. Nobody is the same; there is a difference in levels. Some have a level of being higher than others. It gives them the capacity to work hard, to struggle, to fight. If that person then finds an inner reason they may have a better chance than another.

We take success and failure as part of our outer life. Success for a person who is working is anything that strengthens their attention and gives them more possibility. We have to spend a long time learning exactly what our situation is.

Try to find an aim throughout the day with your various jobs. One can have an aim for what one is doing immediately as distinct from one's real long term aim. It means that whatever task one is going to undertake, however short term or simple, one would try to visualise one's aim. Try to see that in doing this I can decide how I will do it and that I do it for myself. I can see if I try this that there is a tremendous advantage for my inner self about how I approach even the smallest task. It also means of course that for a moment I have to put aside dreaming and this makes me aware of what can take its place.

It is interesting to see that however small or large an aim, the Law of Seven, the Octave, comes into it. It is that first interval that you have to get over. You'll see time and time again, if you can keep your attention and your aim, that if you can get over that first interval, then you find that there is quite a difference in the way things happen. It comes to the next interval, which is something else. This applies to absolutely everything. An aim for your outer activity can come from your inner side, and that's the important thing. Making that decision, however small, when it comes from the inner part of oneself, means that what you achieve as a small outer aim, is really far bigger. From the point of view of improving your inner quality it is important to have attention, isn't it? That is the important thing. Every single thing we try to do, we try to strengthen that. So if you have an aim and you get three quarters of the way through it with your attention isn't that better than not to try? If you struggle and struggle you may fail and fail again, but you are really succeeding in one sense, if you are strengthening your attention.

If you can be really aware, you can say to yourself whatever you are going to do, however simple, 'I can dedicate this to my being'. I have my head, I have my feelings and I have the mechanism that really works my body. I will try to bring these into the operation and then with this resolve, aim and wish, something else in you can take part.

'I dedicate this to my being'. It is possible, in fact, to work with a prayer.

It is like the drunken man—his aim is to get home, just around the corner, at the end of the long street. At the moment it is as much as he can do to get from lamp-post to lamp-post. To reach each successive lamp-post is an aim which requires calculation, effort and optimism.

Acceptance

To accept something in the way we talk about acceptance means that you take it in, swallow it. You have to accept it in such a way that it becomes part of your understanding. What is hard to accept is that the situation is a fact, not that there is something wrong with it. You can know that you have a particular characteristic for example, which is always a barrier for you when you want to work. From your observations you have seen something of this, you've begun to realise that you actually know that about yourself. So you see it over and over again and one day you really see it quite differently and, at that moment too, you accept it. You see how it affects all the other things about you. You take it in and you swallow it with all its implications. Then that changes something inside, but this change doesn't come in a blinding flash, it comes bit by bit.

If I am constantly anxious about which way I am going, what I am doing, all I'm doing is feeding this outer part of myself. You can see how this emotion is emotional energy, just pouring out of me, blinding me, stopping me from seeing, so that it seems to cut me off. But that very energy is what we see with, not this head up here. *That is the energy we see and understand with,* yet most of it is being eliminated, is being wasted, because we are not working properly.

I feed the inner part of myself and in doing that I cease to feed all the negative side of myself, the negative emotion, the arrogance, the attitudes, the opinions, the entire luggage I carry around with me. This work is parabolic, it goes round like that. I don't try to kill anything, I try to feed something inside with the energy that is normally going outside.

You also have to accept the fact that you can never win in this situation, but you gain because of your struggle. You have to make a completely different kind of effort. It's not an effort which says 'I'm going to win, I'm going to gain,' but effort in a sense for almost no reason at all. No strings attached. It is just effort of a completely different nature, because you are not living at the level which you normally live at when you try—make that effort, you are trying to live on another level. Therefore, in a sense, the rules are different.

This is very difficult but once you get the taste of it, once you begin to understand it, you will see that you do it in quite a different way. You don't do it to succeed. You just do it because it is called upon you, it's essential for your way of living, a real way of living.

All of this, what is sometimes called personality, all this outer part of ourselves, actually belongs to life. In other words life is in us, this outer life which is completely out of control. If, by observation, by my work, I begin to see this and almost isolate these little I's within myself, they become, possibly, one single *'observing I'.*

Up to that point it has resisted all efforts to do anything about it because it doesn't want to die. We talk of it dying, we talk of a second birth, but it doesn't die in the sense that it goes away; in fact, it transfers all its energy to the inner part of myself.

You can accept the concept that there is something inside oneself which is of a different substance, a different nature from this frenetically active 'outside' with which we live all the time. To be silent, really silent, means that I feed that inside part. So if, in fact, I could be silent it would eventually know what I want to know. It would eventually begin to change its substance to being something quite different. You have to feed it. To be silent, to be quiet, is not just a flopping exercise, it is a very definite effort of channelling energies in a particular direction.

Asking for Help

A. Yesterday evening I was on the edge of going down a familiar slippery path, struggling with self-pity and anger. I tried to let myself be empty and ask for help. The answer came quite soon and was simple and practical. I see that no amount of thinking will help me. In times of difficulty I must be still, empty and receptive.

That is the crux of the whole problem. We are either turning over and over in our head or feelings, in which case we are not here, we are taken, we are being sucked dry. Or we can withdraw from that and be still. So that's all you need to know, it's obvious. But for each one of us there is some particular obstacle at any given point, and that is my work. Every swami, every teacher will tell you the same thing, all religions say exactly the same, *be still.*

It is very easy to ask for help, and kind of cast oneself on the water so to speak. Yet that is not really the way. It may help in some sense, it may get rid of some of the tension inside. The real way is to realise that one has to go inside and the help comes from the change that takes place inside. The moment I become different, my substance becomes different. The emotional energies are different, of a higher level. This is really remembering yourself. This is what changes all that has gone before, this is what makes the possibility of what is to come. Before I can receive help I have to be helpable.

You have to realise all the time that nothing of any value can happen on this level. The change in level is what makes the difference. It is this change in one's spiritual metabolism which changes what has gone before and enables one to lose the threads that drag you back and hold you where you are.

We know that I can't do anything unless I have the energy to do it. Being quiet, moving away from the outer business which goes on all the time can only be done if I can find the energy to move away from it. Moving away, with the ability not to struggle provides a certain level of emotional energy which feeds understanding. Struggle on this ordinary level is always futile.

That is what I have to die to—the continuous belief in this world. The hardest part to realise is that one is so much in the grasp of imagination, and this is what stops one having understanding.

So I stress always, whatever you do, try to do it with the realisation that you are struggling against, not just an outside world, but struggling against the bit of you that is in the grasp of the outside world, because it is exactly the same. That world is here inside us. This is what you live with.

It's no good just pushing it away. I am trying to push X with X. I have to find energy of a different kind.

I pray. Now if I pray in the mechanical way, purely imaginatively, I will in fact very often feel better. Some people would justify this because they say that their situation changed. Well of course it did. It changed from there to there. No real change at all; just the substitution of one dream for another. You have to find a different kind of energy.

To begin with it can be to a certain extent, imagination. Then you realise it has to be different. This is where the higher level of emotion comes in, which comes through *wish*. You know the power of wish, which wants a bar of chocolate or something, a new dress. It will hold you completely for a very long time until it gets its way. With observation and with increased understanding, you can find that there is a reason for a different kind of wish. That one doesn't want to be the same kind of person, that one wants to change, wants to move, any kind of internal change, then you find a different kind of wish.

So if I had that possibility I could call it *will*, and say, 'I will do this.' But if I can't do that I have to fall back on *wish*, knowing that *wish* is not going to be as powerful as *will* eventually will be. It is matter of knowledge and understanding you see.

Try to bring all this in and practise too. One accumulates understanding when one *wishes*.

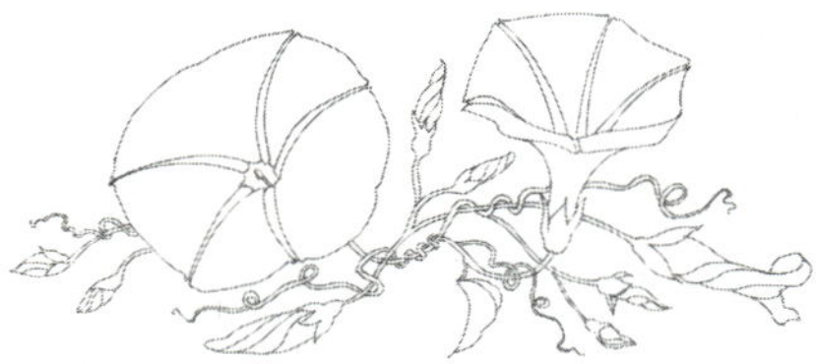

I first came to the group through two members who used to sit and drink at the bar where I was working as a barmaid. When we became friends I was attracted by the way we could be comfortably quiet together and the quality of that feeling of peacefulness that came from them. It was a taste of something I needed and I wanted more. I was also struck by a certain calm and lack of reaction in some situations where most people would have got angry or annoyed—this made a definite impression on me.

When I came to my first group meeting in Norfolk there was again this experience of stillness of all those people sitting together, now more intense than before and it was something I just wanted to drink in. I knew that this was something real and I had a thirst for more. It was new and yet it was like coming home, something I really wanted.

I still have a very special memory of the first Workday I came to and the way the presence of that day remained with me for days afterwards. Working together as a group we can create something that is not possible alone.

Being part of this group has given me a different perspective on life. It has given me a real aim and purpose and has allowed me to see my life, and also that of others, with more objectivity and understanding. Knowing myself has helped me to become more open to influences that can take me further.

Wish

J. When you talk about wish has the word conscience got anything to do with it?

Conscience is a state in which I *see and feel completely* the depth of sleep in which I exist. At that moment, in desperation, I can find the need and strength to wish. The body from which *wish* comes is a possibility. I can't get wish out of the air. It has to come from me, and I have to understand how it can be manufactured. If I have the body of wish, I don't think 'I will have the body of wish'. I just have it. If I have the body of *will*, I don't think 'I will have the body of will'. I just have it.

It is not a vague imaginative thing. It is not 'I want' or 'I would like'. It becomes an actual particular kind of aspect of oneself, an aspect of one's inner self because it doesn't belong to the outer part of you. So you see, when you are practising this—as I say, no longer an exercise, it has to be a way of life—when you are practising this over and over again, you bring in your realisation of this situation, that there has to be a wish, which is the stage before will. These are particular, almost material aspects that one gets, that one is struggling for. This I say so often: we are not struggling to be better, or bigger, we are struggling to be different. An organism if you like, which has the capability of attention, has the understanding of *wish*, which gives it the possibility of *will*. A completely different kind of substance you see. Life then is something one understands. Like a fish in water, you live in it, and you breathe in it, and you know perfectly well if you were out of it you wouldn't be able to live. Unless, like a fish that has changed itself into a land creature, you can get out of it by being different.

Attention

L. Last week I was hanging the washing on the line and the time came to do the exercise you had given us. I did it and noticed how briefly I held my attention. I'm sure I've seen it before, but this time it made me think a bit further about working. It made me see that working at something like this exercise required more and more effort. Somehow I got more of an understanding of what working means and more of an understanding of how I don't work, or of how difficult it is to work.

You know I've often said that you may see something and say 'Yes I know this', but there is a difference when you accept it. What you're describing is accepting something as distinct from seeing. You see how difficult it is to remember yourself; it is quite different from what you think it is when you first come here. But your understanding has to grow to understand and encompass the idea behind it.

At the last Workday I said that one of the qualities, facilities, talents, whatever you like to call it, we find we are lacking, is attention. We know the concepts of centres, these particular points within us which relate to our thinking, feeling and sensing. These parts of ourselves are usually what you might call sending stations whereas they should be, most of the time, receiving stations. You can check this very quickly by realising to what extent you are aware of what you see, hear and sense. If one's attention can be directed so you see what you are looking at and you hear what you are hearing and you sense what you are sensing then the whole inner process is quite different. Today make a real effort to see what your eyes are seeing, to hear what is coming in through your ears, when you walk be aware of walking through your legs, when you pick up something sense the sense of touch, and as often as you can, be aware of the air that you breathe.

H. A number of times recently the shape of objects and things has switched. Colour and shape seem to have a very strong meaning. It may last as long as a minute and then it feels as though it's been cut off. I want to hold it but it gets to a point as if it's taken enough and there isn't any room for it to go on.

It's just that you haven't got the attention. The energy has gone because it needs finer energy than you normally operate with. It hasn't got enough of the right sort of attention to operate the part of you that actually is on that level; it doesn't have the right fuel. This is where inner relaxation comes in. You just let go; put your attention inside and relax and become quiet and still. But you see how things happen; you get a taste of something and if we don't know anything, or understand anything, it just goes. But if we do understand something, it means we bring more and more effort to it, intelligent effort, not slavery, which means putting my attention into the food octave, to try to understand what it means to try to get that finer energy to feed the finer parts of oneself; the higher intellectual, higher emotional parts. Do you understand?

L. I can see there is a part of me that, although it is hungry, it is also passive, it is not taking me further.

That is the Third Octave. We have attention all the time. We are full of it. The essence of the Third Octave is attention, it goes for plants, animals, everything. It is attention drawn away, do you see? It is attention that is feeding life as distinct from one being able to reverse it and operate the inner mechanism differently. You see, the moment you get it it's pulled out of you. You have the whole of the power of Satan on you the moment you try to reverse that process, until you get above the Third Octave to a different level.

L. So attention is produced naturally as part of the evolutionary process, all my normal functions produce this massive amount of attention which pours out through me? But I have to reverse that situation by creating another kind of attention?

Yes. You see *wish* has to come in. The only thing which creates is the Law of Three. It creates at every level of creativity, without it creativity wouldn't take place. So, I'm full of attention, it is being dragged out of me all the time. I am surrounded by it, by my imagination. I see this attention and try to do something about it and see that I can't. But, if I grow inside something which comes from another part which has a wish, then I can hold that attention and that attention can turn into consciousness.

H. Wish feels like such a refined thing somehow.

Quite a lot of people have a lot of wish and don't know what it is for. They can go through great efforts, climb mountains, start companies, do all kinds of things; there is a wish there and they don't know what it's for. That is why very often you see dramatic changes in people's lives. Sometimes they do discover what it's for and they start talking about seeing God, or a vision. They still then need understanding. You have to see that we are subject to processes all the time. It is as if we go through life like animals, then there is a chance of being a little bit different, then there is a chance of being a real person.

Energy and Attention

P. I have been struggling in the last month or two with wildly fluctuating levels of energy. Physical energy and emotional states, with very strong levels of inner energy too. But in the past month on three occasions I have been lifted out of my state. Also the breathing exercise you gave us. This has felt like a survival kit, or a tool. I know even when I am absolutely immersed in something that I can actually leave the house and go for a walk and turn it back, as it were.

It is extremely unlikely in our lifetime, or the lifetime of any of us, that we will be in the position of being able to keep attention all the time. In a sense, it is not the measure of it, it's the depth, you see. So that when one comes back into life, it hasn't quite got the same bite. You learn to live life and just let it flow over you, because you know what your situation is in regard to it. You know what you have got to fight against and you know from your experiences that you have in fact got something to fight with. There is a difference. You don't experience things with nothing, but with something permanent that you have, which over the years you have begun to make. I had always thought of this situation as that described by Don Juan's Warriors.

One goes on for years and years and years. One doesn't know how to work, where to go, what to do. But when you get to this point you know what you've got to do. You know your enemy. It's clear. Simple. I need attention. I need to strengthen my attention because I can see why I need it. I am, at times, just not quite swallowed up. You've got a clear enemy to fight. You've got one other tool that's absolutely essential. That's wish. Without that we don't get to this point, you see. So that is another tool if you like, that has to be sharpened and strengthened.

I trust you will come to a time when you will not do anything without having sensation in your body, even a hand is something but gradually through practice you can have it anywhere in your body. This is a way of getting energy for one thing or converting energy where you want to, as distinct from it just being pulled out of you. The great deficiency we have when we try to work is our lack of attention, we have to practise it, strengthen it by every possible means. You know that if you have attention in your body, if you direct it there, your attention is not being sucked out of you, you are directing it into your body and a hand fully filled with sensation is conscious. The body completely filled with sensation is aware of itself, it is conscious of itself. So you see what you have to do before you start trying to do lots of things.

We don't really know what attention is, except that it is some form of energy. A very special kind of energy. To get that attention, to turn it into myself I need something else. I need *wish.* Wish you can say can be attention. You strengthen your attention by using it. You are then in a sense breeding consciousness, because you can't separate attention from consciousness. Don't become hooked on words, even though we all do it. If you have enough attention, consciousness, you won't want to know what 'I' is, it will be there. It will '*be*'.

With five per cent more attention than anybody else, you are probably 50 per cent more efficient, just on an ordinary level. So you see really, with what I'm suggesting you've got a lot of questions to pose to yourself haven't you? I want to work, I've got some idea of how to work, so what stops me? If someone from outside were to come and bind your hands together you would rebel wouldn't you? But when you do it yourself …!

If I say that part of ourselves is just governed by life, why should you believe it? It's for you to try to find out surely? So I sit quietly, I try to summon my attention which is pouring out of me all the time, on a particular part of myself. Then I discover of course that for some strange reason I can't do it because some enormous force is saying you won't do that, you will do this, you will react to this, you will react to that, to the sound of something passing, to life, to the moon, anything except that which you wish to do. So perhaps if you really think, you would say, 'well, perhaps he's right after all, can I find out more about this, can I prove this more to myself? He says there is something else inside that isn't like this. How do I find this out?' Wouldn't that be a sensible way to go about it?

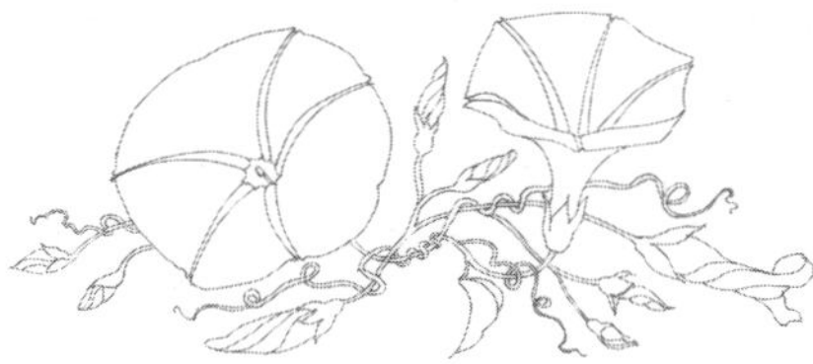

I think when I first joined the group I thought that there would be quick results. One of the things I have had to learn is to accept that there are no fast answers, and that I am where I am, and it is a long process. It is not a question of trying to change myself, but the possibility of becoming something completely different. I have to hear the Work teachings over and over again over a long period of time, and one day, perhaps, I will be listening from a different place in myself, and something will pass into my understanding.

Since I joined the group I have learned the value of trying to be quiet for a while each day, and the remarkable value of visualisation as a preparation for the day. I have learned to work physically with other people, and felt the strength generated by a group of people who are all struggling together with a common aim. I have received wisdom, patience and understanding from my teacher, for whom I feel trust, respect and affection.

Emotion

S. Before I came here this afternoon, I was typing the notes for Sunday and I got to the part, in the morning, when you said 'to feel your emotions with your heart, and to see with your eyes, and to hear with your ears'. What stood out for me on that day was to feel your emotions with your heart. It just struck me that my emotions just live my life, I don't control them, I feel them all over the place.

I had to go and get a book. I don't know why, but I looked at the Food Octave. It's been niggling me over these last few weeks.

Yes, you have to experience. One can have knowledge, but you have got to turn it into understanding by your own experience. It's why we have to spend so much time objectively observing.

You can see how emotion is emotional energy. How it just blinds you, actually stops you from seeing. Seems to cut you off. Whereas that very energy is what we see with, not our head. That's the energy we see and understand with. But most of it is being eliminated, is being wasted. Because I'm not working properly, I don't function as an ordinary thing, I don't function properly.

J. How do I stop negative emotion?

Once a negative emotion starts you can't do anything about it. You see we say over and over again one is asleep—this is sleep. One is mechanical—this is mechanicalness. We have to realise that it is no good trying to talk from the point of view of being conscious, being enlightened, because we are not. You can watch a negative emotion go through to its end but if you could be there for just a split second before it starts then you could do something about it, because you could be in complete control of all these different I's. We have that possibility. But we have to be able to see quite objectively and accept the situation as it is before we can change it. You've had tastes of being different haven't you? Try to see the difference between what we call emotions and what we call the negative use of emotional energy.

The change of emotional energy is the key and when we first begin to get rid of the ordinary baggage we carry around in all the enormous number of different kinds of negative emotions, we then become a little more open a bit to a different level of emotion, we understand quite differently. It is this kind of emotion which is what we need, which does things for us, you see, because up here we have a very high level of emotion which we never normally touch. If I can at times work I can clear the space, I can sometimes just touch it and the amount of understanding from that is tremendous, momentarily.

You have to feed the part of yourself that is quite different, feed this inner part. You feed it with the finer energy which comes from remembering yourself, being aware of yourself.

You know when a negative emotion comes around. It comes in, it goes right the way round and then suddenly it goes away. What's happened? The energy's run out, that's all. It will come back when there's more energy for it. So you can't dismiss it but you need not be with it, you can see it as 'It' and not want to feed it.

It's through our emotional energy that we see, really see, not through our eyes. You've got to be careful not to start looking for another part of yourself with a preconceived idea that it might be there because what you might finally see is just nothing really, or another 'I'. What you must do now is try to prepare in the morning, try to steal a few minutes from each day. Make it a habit for the rest of your life. Try to be as quiet as you can, prepare for the day, do that as much as possible. Try to use your attention to get sensation in part of you, say a hand to begin with.

You see, your ordinary thoughts just go round and round, they are using the energy which just belongs to that particular function. You can't actually change that mode of thinking or behaviour by that same energy. You have emotional energy in another part of yourself, but you have to be present to begin with. You have to make the effort to know that your emotional centre and your head are working together. The energy you have in your head is very slow, the slowest energy we have got. But emotional energy is so much faster, much finer, you see.

Imagination

There are different kinds of dreams, and some dreams come from a different level inside us which can actually tell us something. These are the dreams where we are usually aware of being present in the dream at the same time. But 99.9 per cent of them are just ordinary dreams which have no meaning whatsoever, in fact they are what you live in all day long. If you go on with this Work, as I trust you may, you will discover that you have these all the time, not just at night, and they are in fact what governs your actions and the way you live.

B. Why is that kind of imagination dangerous as opposed to the creative imagination that you have been talking about?

Because we call this being awake! In actual fact we are asleep in this kind of imagination. When you begin to observe this more you will understand it, you will see it. You will see that in fact practically every encounter you have with someone, you may recall it for yourself but not in quite the same way. You are the hero this time. We don't repeat anything accurately, we always put ourselves in a different situation. It's like that for politicians, priests and everybody else, they are all exactly the same. It may sound very unpalatable but it is true. But don't just believe me, find out for yourself.

You see that this imagination which is dragged from us, the energy which is taken from us by life, is on the level of the Third Octave. If I can use my imagination deliberately, visually, it comes to the level of the Second Octave. There you see enormous possibility.

We can be asleep and even in the level of sleep we can still do some Work sometimes. It becomes relative, the levels become relative. So, in fact, you can make energy when you make efforts. Eventually you will be able to use that energy at the time when you understand a bit more.

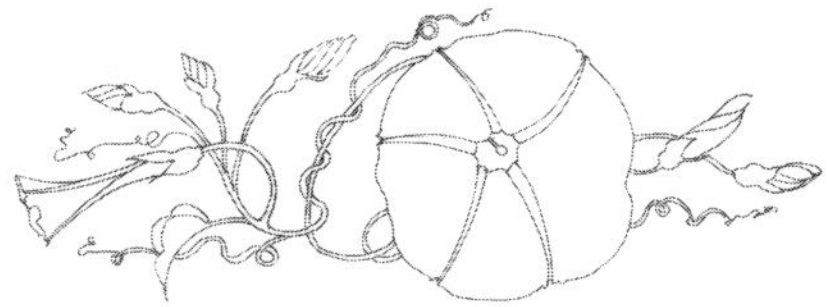

I first met R. at a small public meeting he gave in Norwich. I think that it had been advertised as being for people interested in the ideas of Gurdjieff and Ouspensky. Something struck a chord at that meeting, and at a subsequent one I asked if we could meet more frequently. I was told about the group and started going to meetings in North Norfolk.

I was 25 years old and living totally in dreams, in imagination, in being special. As such I came to the group.

Many years have passed and some things have changed, not only the normal changes associated with 'maturing', but some by the help given from the group. I begin to have a certain understanding of my situation, and from this occasionally an existence apart from a life of dreams. At times I see that it is incredible, miraculous, that this possibility exists. I also see how my laziness and arrogance have hindered me accepting the help offered and made my progress slow.

I am only now beginning to understand some of the things that I was told years ago. Some things which I have been told again and again without hearing are finally connecting.

I have begun to see my dream life more clearly and understand its hold over me. Paradoxically this has weakened its control and allowed the occasional taste of freedom. At times I have seen that my life can be different, completely different, that it has the possibility of being a real life if I can be really there living it

Lying

N. There is something that I have been trying to come to terms with, particularly over the last two or three months, something I've been trying to see. And the more I have been looking at it, the more I've seen of it. As far as I can see, I can't get anywhere until I have come to terms with it.
It is lying to myself, which causes lying to you, lying throughout. I so often think that I've said something that was honest, knowing inside that it wasn't. Time and time again. There is a whole kind of construction built on this.

Everyone's the same. It isn't possible for us to tell the truth because we don't deal in truth. So, it's a fact. But you have to see it is a fact, and accept it. To start getting negative about it is only another form of lying. You've got to see it for exactly what it is, as a fact of the way human beings live. Then, it becomes something different. But you see, you're not accepting it, you're just seeing something terrible. It isn't terrible. It's a fact, neither good nor bad.

Perhaps you will reach a time when the taste makes you so thoroughly disgusted and sick that it's then you begin to work, because you are beginning to see the truth about things. We have a great capacity to lie and to disguise from ourselves that this is the situation. 'I'm really a nice person, I'm just not behaving terribly well at the moment'. You know perfectly well in fact one is not. This is not intelligent. This is a stupid, slavish way of living and we are all in the same boat. But I have the possibility of being different and that is the best thing. But nothing is for nothing. Remember that. Nothing is for nothing on any level. You've got to pay.

This question of lying is terribly subtle and very difficult, but to be able to get to this point, to be able to talk about it is really quite a movement towards something. It is not something you are going to see overnight, it will take years. You can say finally in desperation, 'Can I be without lying? What can I be that is true?' But you will never get to that point without trying to understand the situation and experience it. It is not an academic question.

Try to understand this idea about lying. It isn't easy to understand because there is such a tremendous opposition to us wanting to know anything about it. It enters into the very fibres of one's personality. If it were a matter of just saying 'I am not telling the truth about this' it would be fairly simple to find out about it. But it is firstly not feeling the truth about anything and secondly not knowing the truth about what it is you are concerned with. The Conference of the Birds is about that.

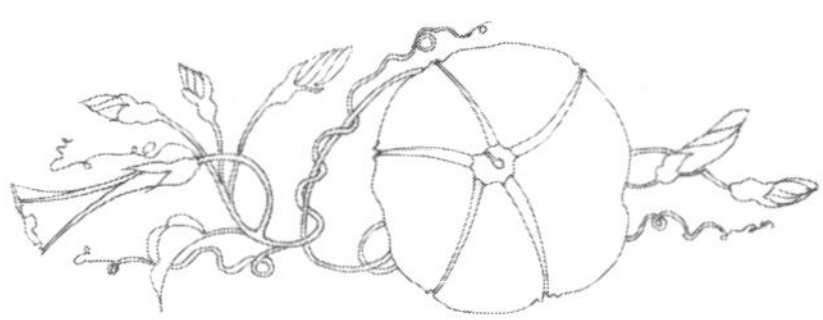

It is easy to drift through one's life using procrastination as a buffer to making an effort. It is also easy to allow oneself to be duped by imagination.

I have seen my laziness and passivity. I have been given the opportunity to accept this as the situation but to exist alongside it, and at times to remove myself from myself and from the force of the Third Octave, to allow another level to enter. If I can do this for only a moment I have found this can change my situation, and if *I can do it I begin to wish for more.*

This is the chance that I have been given; that I can take it or waste it and in the end this is my choice.

Being

A. What is being?

Not easy. The definition I once heard was that one's being is the sum totality of all that one has experienced up to that second. Which does presuppose that you are something that can experience. If you observe yourself clearly you will see that you do not experience much. That is one reason why we should bring up children in a way that enables them to experience as much as possible. It helps the growth of being. Being also is the measure of what one can endure. You can observe that some people cannot endure or apply themselves for more than a few seconds, while some people can last for hours, then you can begin to understand how one's being can be increased. If you are aware, remembering yourself, what you can experience in a second will be an enormous amount. People are born with different qualities of being, some that they have inherited. As Gurdjieff points out, a really good bandit could stand behind a rock for hours waiting and not moving a muscle even with flies biting him. That could be an inherited level of being.

It is a matter of being different. Being different means that whatever you are is changed, but what you have got is what you work on. The fact that the bandit can stand motionless is not going to send him to heaven, is it? If you were able to talk to him about something a bit more enlightened there would be something to work on. As I have said before, we do not take people into the Work who have no quality inside them. Someone referred to as an awkward bastard can be quite good material.

So before you start to do anything, you prepare and you consider that what you're going to do is really a sacrifice, a sacrifice to your being. You have to do it to the utmost of your ability. If a bit is not good, you go back and do it again. When you leave it it's absolutely perfect. And you remember all the time *why* you're doing it like that. Do that for a while, a day, for the whole day and you could, with a bit of luck, learn quite a lot by the evening. But remember why. No fantasy, no imagination, just *why.*

'I wish to be' can be from your emotions. 'I wish to be different' can be from anywhere. So stick to the first one, but try to understand what it would mean to say it as a prayer. It takes a long time to really say it. You say 'I' and try to feel 'I'. What does it mean 'I'? Can I be 'I'? You bring all this in, including the sensation of yourself, as much as possible. And with *wish*—there you go to your emotional centre and see what it means to wish. Is wish just something like wanting a bar of chocolate? Or is it from somewhere else, does it mean something else? What do you need, what's got to be given to you, where can you get this wish? 'To be'. What is 'to be'? What does it mean 'to be'? How do you understand this? How do you feel the idea of being, existing? And so '*I wish to be*' can be a very, very powerful prayer. It's something you have to respect and say with as much intention and as much understanding as you can, whenever you say it.

Respect

J. We speak of having respect, but what do we mean?

As we know, the meaning we give to words is subjective. When we say that we have respect for the law, and obey it, is it because we remember, at that moment, that unless there is an established code of laws there will be no protection for the individual or do we obey through fear, because we might be found out?

We can show respect for an individual for his position, his size, and his uniform—the power he wields. So we can respect a traffic warden, even if he is a low level unpleasant person. But what if we were approached by a traffic warden who we felt emanated the kind of quality which we recognised as being of a higher level, would we have respect for him then? What would that respect be for and where would it come from?

A skilled workman handles his tools and materials in a way which marks him out from an unskilled workman who will neglect his tools and use his materials without care. It is interesting to note that when their work is finished, and they have departed, craftsmen leave something behind with which one is able to recognise their level of craftsmanship, or is it something else? Why should a bricklayer, for instance, take down the last three courses of bricks because he has noticed a slight error which nobody else is going to notice or criticise? Where does the motive for that action come from? His respect for what he does is relative to a standard which is within him. So perhaps we can say that the level of respect indicates the level of being.

Good cooks preparing meals have an innate relationship with the materials they are using. They do not have to measure everything, do not have to examine closely to see whether the materials are good or bad. They know through the fingertips and the eyes and nose; in fact the facilities which come from *essence*. Good gardeners do not use their head when looking to see the needs of a plant, its distress or state of well-being is evident at a glance.

So perhaps we can say there are different kinds of respect, there is that which comes from associated attitudes, a reaction to life situations, and there is that which comes from inside, from essence.

This latter respect is an essential quality for individuals who have chosen to work on themselves. It is more evident in some people than in others. We can acquire it by the way we carry out our daily tasks. To cut a slice of bread with respect means we are aware of the bread and the materials in it and how it has arrived in front of us, of the knife and its ability to cut, and ourselves. Our awareness of ourselves brings a relationship with outside, we then live.

Gurdjieff said if one can make a pot of coffee properly—one can make anything. Try to understand this. A day working together, with the same wish, with respect, can change the level of one's being forever.

Inner Considering

One of the strongest bars of this prison we build around ourselves is called inner considering. The continuous worry we have about how we appear to other people. It is slavery to imaginary fears as we consider what people think of us. Did I do that right? Is my hat on straight? Should I have said or done that? The fears are endless, and groundless, particularly when you eventually realise that others are usually behaving in the same way. Self-observation, objective self-observation, is necessary to bring freedom from such wastage of energy.

B. Why are we so suggestible? I notice this in myself. Recently I was looking at some books in a bookshop and I saw something which was very similar to what I've been working on. I was immediately thrown into despair by this. I was quite shocked, I knew it was ridiculous and yet for the rest of the afternoon I was in such a gloom over it.

I can give you reasons, but they won't stick. What will stick is your own observation of it, again and again and again. Seeing it as absolute fact, not as a distressing fact, or a pleasant fact, but as a cold fact. I end up seeing that I have no initiative, no will of my own at all. That is the only way it will change. I remember at one of the first meetings I ever attended the teacher saying 'we think that we live our own lives but it is probably the last cigarette advertisement we saw'.

B. It's almost as if one wants one's moods, one's fears, brought up.

Yes exactly. Have you noticed that one really hates to be alone, one hates being in a position where one is not being coerced, or dreamed by some means or other. That is why so many people don't do anything without the radio on, or music or something else. They are frightened of being alone. The other reason is really that the part of you which is like that is the greater part of you. It is the part which is absolutely mechanical and it is exactly the same as outer life, exactly the same substance. So you respond all the time to its attractions, its propositions, you are completely reactive to it. Not until you see this completely can the other part of yourself begin to grow, the part which is independent of that and which belongs to a much higher level. Now that of course is quite a big statement, but it won't mean anything until you have seen it over and over again. And this is what Work is. Why can I not be an individual, making my own way, choosing my own path, doing what I wish? Why I can not is my Work. I want to see this.

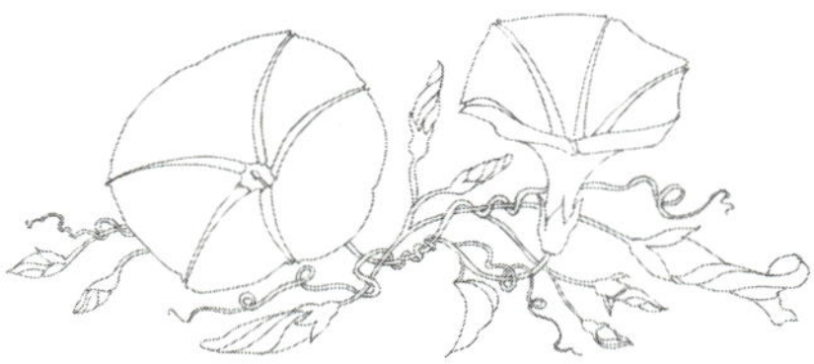

When I joined the group in 1989, my partner had been going to meetings for some years, and I had begun to realise that I needed help in order to direct my life in a more meaningful and positive way.

The work of the group is now a most important aspect of my life. Although I regularly despair that I am making any progress, the practical techniques which I have learnt are now essential tools which I try to use as often as possible in the hope that they will increase my self-understanding and that of the world I live in. I feel that I have gained some insight in this way over the years.

Occasionally I feel lifted out of my 'driven' and self-absorbed life to a calmer and more objective perspective from which I can better accept my situation and have the energy and wish to work further. It has been some time now that I feel I have no alternative but to struggle to be awake.

I also feel that I am taking more responsibility for my life through understanding.

Sleep

L. Last Sunday you mentioned that I was probably inner considering while I was working in the tunnel. I hadn't been aware of that at all. I thought that I'd been working on the exercise. I was dimly aware of inner considering going on which I hadn't been aware of before, and I haven't been aware of since, but which is no doubt going on. You have also said how I throw things away and did I realise that. I see it now, but I hadn't realised it.

It just seems that not only am I asleep, I appear to be in a total black-out. I just can't see any way out of it. I just can't see anyway round it, or how I even begin to pull myself up out of it.

We come here to try and see that we are in fact really quite asleep, utterly mechanical. That is what we need to see, it is all we have to see, but it's very difficult. It's no good saying 'Oh, I see I'm asleep there and I must be awake over there'. Being awake is a very relative term. To begin with it means being awake enough to see that one is asleep! *Not* being awake full stop. That's something quite different.

There is no way forward until such time as you can really see that you're asleep and accept it. You will find, I trust, eventually, that there is some particular aspect of your make-up, which helps to keep you asleep Something about which you revolve. One has to get close to that and then see it, completely. Then accept that. Then talking about being awake can mean something quite different.

L. I've found that I've been very irritated by my children and I think that what they're doing is sort of impinging on my sleep in the sense that I don't want to come out of this sort of sleep. Another thing I felt was that I try to make efforts and perhaps gain some energy and I'm losing it so quickly through this irritation. Last Wednesday I wasn't able to come, but I felt very much that evening that I was with everybody and I had a lot of energy and then it just disappeared with this continual irritation that seems to be connected to this sleep.

Everything is. But you see, to see that, to say we really understand what we mean by being asleep, is very difficult. You don't really see it. You see little bits of it here and little bits of it there. We have to see the absolute situation, the enormity of the fact that the whole of our life is concerned by thoughts, feelings, actions; all of which go to bolster up something we call ourself. And the sole object of that, it would appear, is to stop us putting any attention whatsoever in another part of ourself which is really quite real and which has been starved of attention for years.

So, you're not going to be able to change that overnight are you? What I suggest you do is to try and get some space each morning, some time. Be as quiet as you can, and just prepare to observe and take what comes through the day. You may find that something stops you keeping awake, stops you remembering yourself, perhaps something of which you've just spoken. So you make a resolve about that, maybe for a day, maybe for two or three mealtimes, but try and keep the whole thing variable. Try, and keep it alive. You'll discover, you could discover, ways of working for yourself, which we have to do in the end. The most important thing is to try to spend some time trying to remember yourself. And try to really understand and study what that means. Because if you do take the opportunity then what you know and understand at the beginning will be very little compared with what you can understand at the end. It can be quite different. But if you only set out vaguely to do something for that particular period you will stay exactly as you are. Remember you have intelligence, you have the ability to think and to feel. The use of these is a proper function.

Struggle

I've used the term *'to be a working person.'* To be someone who works. To be that is quite different from an ordinary person. The act of working, the act of struggling, the act of fighting, is in itself something that changes us. One doesn't have to succeed. It is that struggle, the friction that comes from that, which goes to deposit something inside us. We tend to think all the time of doing an exercise or something 'I didn't do it well' or 'I found it difficult.' The Work is what you do and when you try to do something it's very hard to lose this idea of failing. We don't fail, we just don't succeed, that's all. It's not a matter of success and failure, it's a matter of you try something, you try it again, that's all. It's the effort that counts. I don't mean in a moral way, I mean the effort counts in that it has its own results.

Making the effort to be present means that you accept that there is something out there which doesn't want you to be present. You go against all that, but you're being taken and dragged. This can be a form of suffering if you like but I think one could use the word effort instead. Suffering for us has a certain connotation which is not necessarily a good one.

We have to start working quite differently, to start working like grown-ups. We should no longer be people coming up in the Work. We have to stand on our own two feet, really face what it means to think, and look at the facts about ourselves and about everything else as well. We still insist on living in a world of fantasy. It is not easy and it is not pleasant when you really do see how you're walking through a world of fantasy. I've been ill for the last five or six days and it occurred to me today, I feel as if I've been on an excursion into the world of the Third Octave and

I'm struggling to get out of it because I had so little energy—so much of my energy has gone. It's just a kind of jungle.

There comes a point when you start realising that there is a struggle and that struggle eventually seems to be directed by somebody really consciously trying to get at you. It's quite remarkable. You have to realise that you are dual; one side belongs to life, of the *same materiality as life*. The other side, which has been neglected for the greater part of your existence, is beginning to grow and the struggle begins to be evident. But without the struggle there is no progress, struggle creates a particular kind of energy which you need.

J. It was a glorious day and I went out through the woods. I spent a lot of time thinking about trying to be aware of, or just focusing on, impressions which you had mentioned a few weeks before. I found it all very helpful, it gave some space, some time to think about it, but when I got home I thought should I have pushed on with my struggle to finish my sewing. I kept having this quandary about whether I should have struggled on.

One way is to do a deal with yourself, like doing your sewing. You know that you like going outside, then say 'I'll go outside and leave the sewing here but I will come back and I will finish it even if it takes me hours'. You can try that, you've got to learn for yourself many tricks and techniques to cope with life.

Self-importance

M. What is meant by Madame Vanity and Monsieur Self-Love?

What really rules this life is this body isn't it? The emotions, the thoughts, the feelings, they are all part of this body. We tend to think it's something different, but it is not so. In fact that is the function of this particular body. To live in life and provide Nature with enough energy as a result. We have something inside, some of us, which is different, from a different source, from a different materiality, and it has the possibility of growing and living differently from this body. See it like that. See it simply as that. See I have to be there, not here. But I know what goes on and I accept what goes on, and really try to understand what goes on. But I know that part of my possible wish is not to be of that body, but to be of another body which can say 'I' quite differently from the way I say 'I' to every little thing that comes along. If one carries out this way of life one should be able, in the middle of that, to say 'I' and know that it is not that 'I'. It's different.

We say 'I' all the time. Try to see it as 'It'. 'It' wants its own way. If I really succeed in unifying something inside myself, feeding this real 'I' and making it strong, what's going to happen to all the others?

If I succeed in finding this stability and feeding this inner part of myself, firstly those outer I's are going to rebel because they do not want to die and they know that that is their fate. This is not a new idea. Christ talked of it frequently. Wouldn't it be nice to be able to see all those Gadarene swine and dismiss them?

Every philosophy, every religion comes down to the same thing, the importance of self is what ruins our possibilities. This is the sleep, the dreams and the selfs which react to all the influences from outside to keep us chained up. With experience, with intent, we can see this. The question is then, what do we do about it? As I have said before, if I can be quiet, if I can put my attention on the real part of myself, then that is enough, I will discover all that I need to know. But when I try to do this I find that for a moment, a minute even maybe, I can do it, then something takes me away. So see that what takes me away is my Work. This I see by absolutely objective observation. What is it that stops me doing what I wish to do?

Try to see that it is a fact that one is so concerned with oneself and this is self-importance. It can be that self or this self or another self, it's still self-importance. But you can be aware of another self inside which is different from the ones that you are surrounded by which react to all the different things which come in. Instead of self-importance say 'importance of self'.

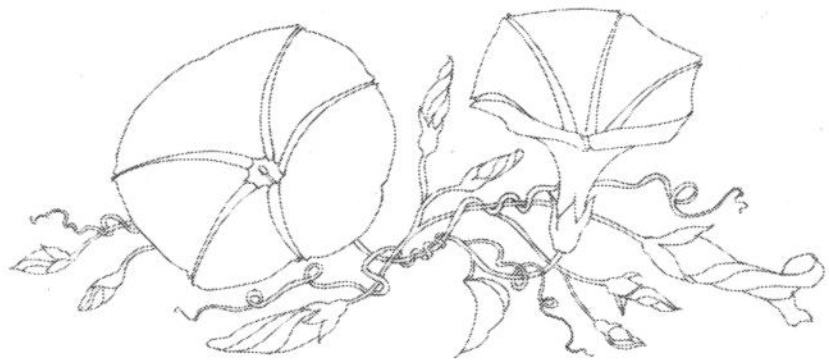

Some friends through the group introduced me to R. I found a way of making sense of life. Until I became familiar with the ideas in the group I had no understanding how life worked or my place in it. I began to see more clearly that I am part of something that is not purposeless, that is intelligent and that I am able to trust. This has enabled me to taste some freedom and this is now my pursuit.

I have received a chance to grow up. Where before there was only confusion and nothing to build upon, there is now a direction and increasing comprehension of the way things are. I am thankful.

Death and Rebirth

I suppose some of you probably consider Christ a fictional character. Some of you, probably, consider him just a myth. Some of you may consider he was real individual, who went through a particular political manoeuvre or somebody from a higher level who went through great suffering.

In a sense it doesn't matter what you think. What is very important is the parable which is passed down. The parable of birth following death. If you read, study past history, past mythology, you'll find this comes up over and over again. Prince Gautama lived in a palace as a boy, shielded from all outside life. All he was able to see was what was good. He happened upon the outside life and saw exactly what the situation was. Then spent his life trying to show a means for coping with it for other people. The same parable. You'll find it happens over and over again.

How does this apply to us, how does it apply to me? Birth following death is happening all the time isn't it? If you begin to observe yourself closely, once you really begin to live with your inner life, you'll see that it is a process going on over and over again.

We meet the Work and we become aware of all our attitudes and opinions that we carry around with us. With a bit of clear observation one day we see some little thing and it dies; in its place there's the birth of a little understanding. It's a process which goes on and on if we continue to work. There is of course, for us, the possibility of this 'I', which we create when we observe ourselves and all the little separate I's are united in that 'I', dying too, with the strength and experiences accumulated being born in our *'real I'.*

We are told this Work is difficult, we are told that it is almost impossible, but in actual fact we do begin to change. That change comes from something which we acquire inside. It's a materiality which we acquire inside, of a different substance. That, of course, also brings its opposite in the resistance experienced because the greater part of us does not want this to happen.

When we make the change, something is reborn, and this new birth is the change of all this that we call personality. This then gives up and the strength it has goes over to the other side, our inner life. We are told that it has to die, but it doesn't die in the sense that it disappears; it ceases to be active and its strength goes to the inner part of oneself.

Unless there is that possibility it doesn't seem to me that there is much point in being here. The alternative to the Work is a wooden overcoat which contains nothing that has any future except to go back to the earth as compost, which is again part of the equilibrium.

This rebirth is not something that I can just reach by aspiring to it or wishing for it. I reach that level by the change in my being. In other words, in almost every case I attract my possibility.

Try to see this, the potential for development of something inside. There's a magnetic centre created so that my effort becomes quite different. You can make tremendous efforts, which are just slavery, or you can make efforts with understanding and intelligence. Consciousness attracts and creates inside oneself something of a different substance.

Observation from Tokyo

K. When I first arrived here there seemed to be a separateness from what was going on around, something appeared to be watching what was happening. I remembered thinking it might be different here or maybe I was hoping as always that K. would be different. But of course that feeling of distance rapidly disappeared to leave all the usual inner considering and baggage, everything I always take around with me. Very familiar, just different surroundings.

I saw some of them more clearly maybe because everything is newer out here or at least there weren't ingrained habits to protect it. For a short while I could see more clearly that K. was K. and always will be, and there is always a strong emotional reaction to seeing how I am … disgust or despair at what I see, which only adds negativity and increases the inner considering.

Just occasionally, rarely, there is the process of just seeing it and that is all.

The strong reaction there has been that, when in a sea of people in the middle of Tokyo, I see the sleep of so many as a reminder of my own. In moments of awareness I have a feeling of just how small and insignificant I am, and that is just in this world. With that comes the questions, how and why did I come upon the Work. Then I have a feeling of great responsibility, and I know this has been mentioned many times, enormous gratitude, at being shown what to do.

Responsibility to what or what for eludes me. Or I can't, as I am, answer such questions. Most disturbing is that this doesn't spur me on to work.

I am finding it very difficult to be here, as you warned us. There is a lot of thinking about things, people in Norfolk, lots of imagination going on, but no doing. Activity but no action.

Meeting 1

L. The gap between how I would like to be and how I actually am seems so wide. I try and visualise and every time my reaction, when the event comes, makes me think of St Paul, 'That which I would, I do not, that which I would not, that I do'. Yesterday was a difficult day, the battle of forces inside had a Martian quality, very creative and simultaneously very destructive. I felt I had absolutely nothing. I had been feeling that there was something stronger inside me but there was just nothing, I couldn't ask for help, nothing, and again that is in contrast to what I wish.

You have to be careful not to fall into the trap of thinking that, because you are in a very bad state, the opposite of that is something good. What you are after is something different. You can go on for years thinking like that. There is no point in being the better of what you already are, you have to be something different.

This is the great mistake made by all kinds of groups, people who promise you this and that. It is not a matter of being better than what you are. It is nothing to do with that. You have to be of a different nature, a different substance. That comes from the effort, the friction, and the struggle inside of work. But if you get a fixed idea that you have got to be better than what you are now, it is exactly the same thing, you are on the same level. You have to be on a different level. There is no virtue in being better than something on the same level. This is hard to understand but you have to see it is a change that has to take place.

L. Something that seemed clear was the feeling that I don't want anything from external life. I asked you recently about this need to express, to manifest. I have struggled with this, but I think the answer is to try and make something inside.

Yes. Firstly, one has to wake up what is inside. Then one has to feed it, look after it. It is the understanding which makes this difference in level. The recognition of the possibility of making something of what we have inside is what brings the beginning of any change. You say that you do not want anything from outer life; you can't really say that, because we have to live in outer life. What you can say is: that I want something for this inner part of myself. Not just always for the outer part.

You see, we can't actually do anything in the sense of manipulating or turning knobs, we can only move towards a wish, towards a different level, to open ourselves rather that just grasping something. When I get this utter acceptance of myself, this understanding that I am powerless to do something, it doesn't mean to say that I have no possibility. My acceptance of my powerlessness to do anything is the beginning of my possibility. I then move away from my obsession with being better rather than being different.

L. I think the thing with the outer life is that I make demands. My relationships are not clean with people. I am somehow extracting, demanding. I don't want to have to be like that.

Well, that is a matter of technique, using one's intelligence to live one's life a little more easily. I want to work. Anything that I can do to make that easier for myself is to my advantage. But you will find that you cannot do that to anybody else's disadvantage.

N. Is that because you would be anchored by your conscience in some way?Suppose you chose to shirk some responsibilities in order to give yourself some space to do work or to sit and be still.

If you did that or thought that was what you were doing, then some kind of struggle would take place inside, and the debate would do it for you.

N. Do what?

Change the situation. You see we have to be something different and what you are saying is still on the level of being good and bad. It isn't like that.

If I try to make my life better for my inner work then I take into account so many different circumstances. It isn't a matter of being solely selfish, it is a matter of manipulating so many things. I may have to go considerably out of my way to make it possible for me to do something within the realm of somebody else's life. I would have to go to great lengths to help them in some way.

Think about it. If I want to withdraw from somebody, I can't just withdraw, there would be results. I have to find a way of withdrawing that doesn't have any repercussions. I have in fact to start being clever and playing the game in all ways. As I read the other day, an Indian person talking about meditation: 'First you find a place free of insects'. What do you do about them? Kill them? There will be more.

A. After lunch on the Workday I felt a strong feeling that there was a possibility. It felt as if it was something that I could trust, that it was actually from somewhere. It was the only thing that seemed real. You mentioned that there was a spiritual heart and I don't know if it was imagination but something touched me inside. Is a spiritual heart something that has always been there or is it something that we grow? Is it the beginning of another body?

I think it is part of another body. I do not think it is there for everybody. I think it has to be grown and nurtured. It is part of something that can be quite different in your life.

A. I have been trying to come back to it through here (indicates chest) and I am still not sure if it was imagination.

It is not imagination because I remember the actual moment when I said that and I saw you. It is something you have to work at.

P. At the movements last week, I had some time when I was struggling with something that I do not usually struggle with. The usual stuff seemed not to be there. What was there was mine and it seemed so much more beautiful and worthwhile than the stuff that I normally struggle with all the time. It was real.

Yes I understand.

P. It was as if I had something to hold to that would not fall away, for that moment.

This is the kind of struggle that isn't concerned with success or failure, but a struggle for its own sake.

P. I saw since then that there seems to be a connection for me, between fear and arrogance. They appear to be two ends of the same stick which lead nowhere and have nothing to offer me. Why are they connected?

At one end of the stick is the fear of emptiness, of not being able to submit but wanting to, yet not being able to. The fear of the emptiness of my selfish self. At the other end is the arrogance, which fills up the emptiness and puffs it out whenever it can. Between these two ends is a marriage which seems to spawn all the devils which take my attention all of the time, and they are all fraudulent.

And the fear is just protective of all my little I's. So are most fears.

P. How does one let go of them?

By looking at it objectively more and more. You begin to see the situation, when you really see it is the only way to deal with it. The more one struggles to see, the more one has the possibility of seeing and the more one actually creates a seeing I, which becomes more permanent.

The existence of that begins to change the situation. The fear of emptiness is something which everybody comes to, and the paradox is that as long as there is the fear of emptiness there is no room for anything, we are blinded from seeing what could be there. You have to accept that we are not going to find something completely ready-made, what we find is a potential, a possibility. Which of course is marvellous. Our fear just prevents us from reaching that potentiality.

J. Everything you say today seems to make me cry. It is extraordinary.

It is a certain level of energy.

J. I have been thinking about speaking and how to speak without being full of self-love; it is difficult … impossible.

L. I got the book by Rodney Collins, The Theory of Celestial Influence. I read that just everything is connected, everything on every level, from the coarsest to the rarest, the most dense to the highest energy, in every direction you look, up, down, sideways, front, back, in my life, outside there, up there. The whole lot is interconnected, interpenetrating.

I see that I am just a pawn in a game. Yet even though through reading this I got the feeling that although everything is like that and I am not in control in any way whatsoever of my life or what I do, I haven't found that horrifying. On the contrary, I found that I am part of this amazing process which is just incredible, the most wonderful thing.

Now you understand what I mean by being different. Not better or worse from what one is. You have got a bit of understanding which can only take place if something has taken place inside you.

One of the big causes of the feeling of emptiness is the denial that anything else exists except us.

L. Another thing, every so often my attention has come back to my breathing and one of the things I have been very aware of is how shallow it is each time I put my attention on it. I am obviously not breathing properly like that. Is it possible to breathe properly without attention?

However, last night while sitting listening to a radio programme, I noticed that my breathing was deep and full. Tonight while relaxing waiting for you to come in I was aware of my breathing changing and becoming deep and full without any effort on my part, so is it that one needs to relax and then it will happen? I feel that I do not help myself by having that sort of breathing most of the time.

You have to consider what demand is being made on your breathing at any given moment. If you had to escape from a charging bull you would find your breathing would be quite different. Your body would demand it. Your circumstances do not always need all the breath that could come in. Most people would find that when they have attention they are breathing shallowly. To breathe more correctly from the diaphragm rather than the chest is something you have to come to and you will find it unlikely that you will be doing it all the time. Unless you spend all your life doing that and nothing else.

Do you find that when you put your attention on your breathing that if you try one or two breaths that your body suddenly wants a larger breath?

L. Yes.

That is the answer, something needs more food that comes in with the air. You must remember it is a food.

F. Something you said last time about how my body runs my life, triggered a series of events that has made me understand that a great deal more.

I was reading part of a Bennett book where he was talking about conscious denial. The student concerned had denied himself food for a day. I thought I would try that because I found in my daily practice that whatever I affirm in the morning consistently falls by the wayside.

So I decided to deny myself breakfast and lunch. I am very attached to food and it was difficult. The hunger was a continual reminder, it really helped, it doesn't go away and it helped me to remember why I was doing it. I understood more and subsequently I have been very aware of how my body is completely running my life and how so many things are needed to satiate it in every respect to keep it comfortable. It shies away from any discomfort or effort. Today I decided to try and look forward on the hour to what I was going to do in the hour ahead; that changed my day considerably too. It was something to help me to remember but I let it slip this afternoon.

What is your real purpose?

F. To see my situation exactly as it is.

What do you need to see your situation?

F. Energy.

Attention. That should be your objective, to strengthen your attention.

F. One other observation: the other evening, after movements, I was very fired up by them and was finding sleep difficult. On the cusp of sleep I suddenly seemed to have left myself, I shot out of myself in a funny sort of way. Then the fear struggled back; the fear of it threw me back into my bed. It was the fear that was anchoring me.

You don't have to fear.

Meeting 2

J. I see that I am back at the beginning again, much further back than I would have imagined I could be. I feel it's a more complete beginning than before.

When you say 'beginning' what do you mean?

J. I see that previously I have reached points where a new understanding gives you the insight that you haven't really begun.

It's important not to make the mistake of trying to measure. You say that you have 'reached an understanding', well that in itself is a contradiction in terms, because in the beginning there was no understanding, so it's a change. As I say over and over again it's not a question of being better, bigger, fatter or larger, it's a matter of being different, it's not a matter of being at the beginning or the end at all.

J. I was prompted to say what I said because I see that some part of me has entered into that idea of measuring. I can't say that there is nothing like that this time but I understand that there isn't a part for that.

You see, in the beginning there would be no idea that this Work would be difficult, just an idea that there was something to be done, something to be gained. As one gets understanding one realises that it is not going to be a simple task, there is going to be pain and suffering and that you can't measure your progress by being better or worse. You can have all the ingredients for a cake nicely mixed in a bowl, they can get better than when you started, you can add a bit of brandy to them, but until such time as it's been through the oven, through the fire, no purpose has been served.

B. In my last letter to you I spoke of this strong realisation that I was going to die, and there was something else that went along with that, a breakdown of what I thought was confidence. Also my everyday world changed, I engrave differently, I sculpt differently, there seems to be a change almost as if some veneer came off me.

I understand. As we do become different what happens inside is bound to manifest in one's ordinary life somehow or other.

L. You spoke to me the other day about assenting to something. At the time I was talking about when I tried to sit down to be quiet, and how the thing that I sit down with is something that will only take me so far. And I saw that this business of assenting to something is also a something, a third force, or brings in a third force. You reminded me of Madame de Salzmann's talk about 'A Look from Above', and this business about there being something above but also inside. A little like you were saying to J. just now about having all the ingredients but without the fire, there being only the ingredients. And I can see that I could go through a whole morning's preparation, and go through the whole of being quiet and having sensation, of breath, of attention, and there being nothing without this other thing. This other thing is coming much more at me at the moment, not just when I am sitting down. I find that I am reminded much more to try to relate to something inside myself, to trust something inside myself. The thing that you were talking about was the force of life, the Third Octave. I seem to have moved into it more ... I have always been comfortable in one sense in my life and I am not at the moment, in that the force of life, mostly other people, is making me uncomfortable. I seem to be causing enormous chaos in that, or there is enormous chaos for me, but there is also this other force and the two things are terribly sharply defined at the moment.

The more one increases this inner life the more one becomes aware of the outer life and the difficulties that it has. Without this knowledge or this feeling about one's inner life, outer life just completely absorbs you. You are beginning to separate from it do you see? So one is in the situation that one must feed the inner life and at the same time accept the outer life. The more you feed your inner life, the more your understanding grows, the more you will see that you become separate from outer life. It is all the more important then to accept it, you can't just close the door on it, sit in a cell like you could two or three centuries ago; we now live in a completely different way.

L. Accepting that I am made of that stuff, 99.9 per cent made of that stuff.

So it is a miracle that you can grow something inside that is not like that, but is dependent on it because that is why you are here.

D. I am feeling that I am at some kind of changing or turning point in my life. I can't quite put my finger on it in some ways but I seem to be able to look at my life more objectively than I ever have before. There are things that I want to change, but I haven't done anything about it, but at the same time I seem to be attracting different people coming into my life, different contacts either helping me or the other way round and I relate that to change in some way. I am still finding my energy on the health front not very high but I do seem to be getting more emotional energy that I can't do anything with at the moment. It seems to be there despite a weak feeling overall.

You can see that if one does actually have something inside that begins to grow it has a quality—a completely different substance, so it must in some way or another have some effect, and this is where it begins to manifest in one's outer life. This again is where one really has to begin to understand outer life and accept it; you see it for what it is rather than just its pulls and pushes. You see that, as L. says, you are 99.9 per cent the same materiality.

T. The other day I was thinking about time and memory. I looked in the Reyner book, and it said something about memory, that we are privileged to have memory. For example, looking back at our childhood, how it was all acquired through socialisation. Then when I consider the moments when I get very stuck and wonder what's going on in my life I have a memory of a very simple exercise—just to breathe or have sensation in your hands—and they are just such simple reminders. And as I sit here now it seems that I am only just recognising how simple they are and how much help they are to me now in my life. In relation to my inner and outer life I want to ask a question about that but I haven't got one.

Your question really is 'where does the memory come from?' You see, your body has a memory, your body has many memories in different places but there is also another memory which is of far greater importance. L. also mentioned this too, your body reminds you, it likes having sensation. But with that now comes another memory which really tells you why you want to do this, why it's important to do this with attention.

L. Are there different levels of memory?

Infinite. You see J., this is what we are talking about too, you have to be careful not to cloud what is happening by your tendency to be sentimental about it. By sentimental I mean the way that you usually kind of run things down about yourself. We can change, we do change and it is important to realise when this change is taking place, not to deny it.

S. I have still been trying to carry on looking at aspects of my sleep. One thing that came to me was the fear of having an image of myself which is in fact perfectly empty, quite false, but being afraid of really admitting or understanding that or letting it be seen that that is the case, of sort of holding it out instead of just either letting it be useful in circumstances and getting behind it or just letting it go. I am trying to put this verbally but it is something that came to me without words when I was sitting quietly one time.

What really stops you doing that?

S. What stops me letting it go? Well I'm not sure I know really but something that L. said earlier just struck something here, something about being prepared to trust something inside that just went in. I thought 'You're holding on to that, why don't you just trust something inside?'

Afraid.

S. It's afraid without being afraid of.

Just fear. How many years have you been coming here?

S. Quite a lot now.

I have waited all the time for you to say this. The dervish movement, remember when I tried to make you do it? You see, it doesn't matter that one can be wrong, one can be stupid, one can be all kind of things but you can see that the fear that one has of being like that really rules and cripples you. Just try to be able to let go.

J. Recently I had an expectation of what my life should be like and I realised that I was kind of disappointed and saw that it was something to do with my age and it must happen to everybody. I didn't realise that I had an idea of how things should go and I have begun to accept that that's the way things are. I felt quite ashamed that I was disappointed.

Where does one's idea of what one's life should be like come from?

J. I don't know, I didn't know it was there.

How you are brought up and ideas that you pick up and so on. When you look at it one sees that one has no choice at all in the way we are. A Roman historian once said 'Those who will, the Fates lead, those who won't they drag'. It all comes down to what I said to start with, if you start to create an inner life then you cause complications because you can't just go along the normal way completely absorbed, dragged by the nose. You begin to resent this, and this inner part is really tremendously strong once it begins to grow, it has a tremendous effect on your outer life. This is the important thing, and if you are free to understand that, you will see your life in a different way. You will see it in perspective and you will see that it is utterly, completely mechanical. That's why I say that you have to accept that aspect while you feed and grow this inner part of yourself.

S. I have had problems with my back that have restricted my movements and I noticed how hard it was for me to relax. I saw what the depth of real relaxation means, I saw that I was a long way away from that. But in a way although I was restricted I saw there was another benefit, a bit like D. was saying. My sister has been staying over for a few days and I noticed that we were not fitting into our normal pattern. I felt free from the normal pattern that we always slip into. We were both different, it wasn't just me, there was something that we were both responding to.

You have your roles don't you? Had them for years, so you were slightly jolted out of yours, and she didn't meet the familiar role. Life is just as mechanical as that.

S. I do accept that. Somehow I see the enormity of the task and yet I see how simple it is, it's quite strange.

The enormity is that one has to change. The simple aspect is to concentrate on that and not start fighting it and everything all around you. Many groups nowadays tell you how to do this and how to behave like that and all the time they are talking about life, they are not talking about any other development, any change. They are just talking about being better or coping with life, and there's no point.

G. At the fête this year I had somebody come and sit next to me who wanted to have really quite a nasty conversation. I was absolutely determined to give them no juice at all and I became quite detached really and they went away quite quickly. But almost immediately somebody else came and sat in the same chair that I had never met before, never seen before, who was in great distress. And I think it was because I had become so detached, and also so alert with the first conversation that I could listen to her and I had the feeling that I was seeing past what she was saying, between what she was saying. Her story was actually quite different to the one that she was giving me. I feel that I am somebody who nearly always takes everything at face value so it was quite a departure for me.

Has what I have been saying earlier got any meaning now, about this inner part of oneself? It has much greater discrimination, and of course you would be using a certain amount of emotional energy and it is emotional energy that sees. Normally you are blinded by it, as you say you take it at face value, but detached, that energy can serve quite a different purpose. It is what you see with, what you understand with.

Meeting 3

J. Following the conversation that I had with you the other day, I have seen that my way of seeing things is, again, inadequate. In the first instance, this seems to be one of those times when one peels off layers and layers. In the past I've realised that there's a limit to what it seems to me that I'm capable of and then there's a kind of action which isn't dependent on my thinking or my feeling. I am seeing again that, in a sense, I understand it's important to have a viable position with regard to one's place in the world, one's situation. Much more than that is not only not required but is a burden.

This morning when I sat quietly, because of that conversation—it was less cluttered. I could see how, over a period of time, even though I didn't think I was layering experiences with my muddles, that had obviously happened. And when I try to prepare in the morning, most of the time is spent trying to leave that rubbish behind. This morning it seemed easier because I'd seen that my current way of looking at things isn't viable, if you like. That was a long way round the houses. I don't have—perhaps it's not necessary—a way of understanding or thinking about these ideas.

Why is it a burden?

J. It can be a burden in my case when it becomes just muddled.

But you spoke as if this was a burden generally. As if it's a burden that you understand.

J. I guess I'm wondering if it's even necessary to have what is no more than opinions about ideas. For example, we started to talk about mind and that there are different minds. I was still thinking in terms of a level which was my normal mechanical kind of level. And then there was a something beyond that which I could occasionally peep into and then come back to my ordinary level. And I had assumed that it was important to have a reasonable basis in this ordinary level—just a platform—which would allow those journeys to this other part or the effect of the other part to be more noticeable or more often. So that was my little inner scenario that was padded out with various experiences. For some reason or other, from the way that you spoke last week–we spoke about dreams–all that seemed to disappear, and I saw that was a kind of baggage which seemed to work for a while and now, for some reason or other, doesn't work so well.

If you're in the sea you've got to be able to swim, haven't you? You're in life; you've got to be able to live it. The greater part of the first few years of the Work are spent in getting one's ordinary physical body—this whole make-up, this whole set-up—balanced. So it's necessary. It's necessary to be able to live life efficiently, to cope with things. But you said it could be a burden. It's quite true. So what makes it a burden? Excessive attention put in that direction, excessive energy going in that direction.

J. I would say almost belief in it.

I think you've got to be able not to believe in it. It's rendering unto Caesar what is Caesar's. But not more than what is due. You have to be efficient in life.

J. I'm trying to apply that to what I feel about it. Perhaps it's no more than that. No less than that.

You see other experiences—experiences of a psychic nature or spiritual nature—can take place in two situations, as far as this body is concerned. One is completely damaged, and lives experiences through damaged senses which don't really mean anything. Or it can be through properly balanced bodies which have had experience in knowing how to have experiences, if you like. But the essence of all proper experiences is that they have been paid for. This is the way the Work works. As I've told you before, you can get certain experiences through drugs but they disappear because you haven't paid for them, you see.

J. Yes, that makes sense. That went home.

You see what you and Jn. were talking about—this dream about nature—was the kind of experience I have been trying to encourage in you by visual imagination and by, at certain times, putting yourself back here or wherever; in other words, the use of the second body.

You can say that the world which is inhabited by mind or minds is the real world and when we can, at times, deeply remember ourselves, we touch that world as well. You notice how things appear different and one sees detail you don't normally see.

J. That's a distinctly different experience from the occasional alterations that occur as one balances oneself, I presume. Unless there's some similarity. Is that the same thing?

Remember what I said. Remembering oneself is the blending of the energies of the head, the feelings and the body; in other words, the three centres. The energy going in a proper direction rather than being dispersed as normal.

A. For a long time now I really haven't been able to do anything at all and for a while I was able to hide this from myself. I'm completely powerless to do anything. I really have not the wherewithal at all. I have no motivation and I really haven't a clue what to do about it.

Has anybody in the group got the power to do it?

A. No, but some people seem to be able to do more than just turn up from time to time. In terms of making an effort, I feel like my first weeks here—back in the first weeks as part of the group.

Yes, I too at times, you see, have spent quite a long time like this. But, in a way, it is separate from the actual Work one does. J and Jn. had both experienced dreams which were somewhat similar but were definitely not the ordinary kind. Neither of them could really understand it and one in fact was really quite scared about it. The kind of dream they had was the result perhaps of years and years and years of little bits of Work. He would certainly say he hadn't put in much effort because for years, as you know, he didn't come. But once this Work begins, it goes on inside oneself. The fact that we don't seem to be able to make an effort is seeing the nature of what kind of effort is required, what part of oneself has to make that effort. The other part of oneself can never make an effort.

A. No, I know.

It comes from somewhere else, you see.

A. But I can't just sit back and wait. I mean I can, I am, that's precisely what I'm doing.

No, I don't think that's true. There's a concern about this?

A. Yes.

What do you think the concern does?

A. Not a lot.

Well, it does do something, you see. A little while ago, when I talked about keeping appointments and things here, you mentioned that there had been an experience about which you spoke. Now that is not possible unless something has happened inside you see.

A. I know in the past that something has happened inside. And it seems like whatever has happened in the past is in the past. There have been certain changes and I know there is a residue of those changes. And, in a certain sense, that's quite dangerous because it's an incomplete process, a very incomplete process. But also I've lost a certain fear. And to have lost that fear is actually very dangerous for me at the moment. My behaviour, in both large ways and small ways, is completely outrageous sometimes. I have no care; I have no concern. That isn't a surprise to me particularly. In the end, I see that my behaviour hurts myself as much as the people to whom I'm doing it. That isn't always very obvious at the time, but I know it to be true. I haven't got the means of doing anything about that at all.

What would you want to do about it?

A. I'd like to be responsible.

The fear that went, did that make you appear to be more responsible?

A. I don't know.

As I see it, from what I've seen, when you lost certain things, you became more of what you really are. There was a certain self-restriction in the way you behaved and your behaviour became the behaviour that belongs to you. Do you agree with that? I think you'll find that will settle down, if you like. You won't change that kind of behaviour because that is what you really are. And that is part of your asset, your strength. What is perhaps of concern at the moment is the lack of restriction which is still a novelty. And you're enjoying it.

This aspect of oneself is absolutely necessary. There's no place in the Work for people who haven't got a very strong outer personality because that is what is later converted. You can't wish this situation away. It will change, in a sense, but outwardly it may appear the same. Inwardly you will find it will be different and you find the hurtful things that you say to people, you can say the same, and the hurt won't happen. Through one's own observation.

A. And it'll change without me making any effort, will it?

I think if you try and change it directly that's not the right way.

A. No, but I need to make some kind of effort.

Seeing that situation is part of the Work, it's part of what's happening to oneself. It's not an academic exercise. It's something that's stirring oneself up inside and one has to go on stirring oneself up. You can't be happy with it. But, you see there's something changing place inside, which one rarely recognises, and one knows that one is changing. But the change is not to make one happy.

A. I understand that. I just don't want to go through the world damaging left, right and centre.

I think you overate that quite frankly. Your manifestation is what is worrying you really.

A. Not all of it. OK, I'll go away and think about all this.

I can say in response to what you say, 'too bad, go away and work'. But what I'm trying to say now to one or two people is to try and see that they have actually changed. We do change, it is possible. It is keeping it within our sights with the understanding of what is really happening. The outer part of ourselves is terribly powerful. And it doesn't want to change. But the part that is manifesting in you now is not that part. It's an inner part, you see, which has been freed but is not yet grown up. I told you on one occasion that you had a part to play in the future, didn't I? That's the part that will play it when it's grown up.

M. It's true that I would like to want—I don't know how to express it—but to do something here, to do something for me, to do something. And it's true that if I then say 'Oh, for God's sake let's just have three breaths, let's try to get sensation, let's try to remember for the duration of going down the steps', I do find it shocking, appalling, because I can't, because I am completely without the material to do that kind of thing. But also because J. described it very well when we spoke the other day: he said we both put on very good clothes, Work clothes. And it's true. I see that. But those Work clothes were damn good, and completely artificial in a fairly fundamental way. But, in other respects, if you gave an idea I sort of knew what to do with it up to a point, and for a small time, I could understand the sensations and movements in the body and so on, and the different energies, and I could imagine that taking place, and sense it taking place. All that equipment, all that material is missing. I just don't have it and I do find that galling. And, if I then say, 'what would I like to want to do', I would like to want to be …

Why is it galling? Because the capable, powerful M. can't do it.

M. That may be part of it. I'm sure it is.

It's 99.9 per cent of it.

M. I suppose it's also this sense of complete waste.

That's the other 0.1 per cent. I told you at a meal we had at your house some time ago that you have something to give up and that it would be very hard for you to give it up. This is what you are finding. It's impossible for you to give it up. Sharma told me a story once about himself. He was with the Ramana Maharshi. One day he told him to go outside and prostrate himself in front of the first person that he met in the street. And he found this terribly difficult. Finally he did it, and he threw himself down in front of someone. It happened to be a very venerable priest who picked him up and hugged him. But he had to give up a tremendous amount to do that.

One has to make a distinction between the regret that one hasn't got the energy to do these little things that we want to do in the Work, and the gall that comes from saying 'I ought to be able to do it, but I can't. Of course, I really am capable of this kind of thing'. One of them is 99.9 per cent and the other is 0.1 per cent. You can't work if you haven't got the energy to do it. To begin with your imagination supplies the energy to do this. The fact that you belong to a group which is spiritual and all this kind of business. And you are carried along by that imagination.

Alright, there's a problem. The first thing to do is to economise in the energy you throw away. This you do by observation. Really try as hard as you can for objective observation of yourself. At those moments, if you really look objectively at your negativity, you will extract the energy from it. It's a great source of energy from this very simple act of objective observation. It's a remarkable bit of alchemy.

Meeting 4

S. I was looking at the Gnosis books over the summer and something that really came home to me was the insistence that faith, hope and knowledge were an indispensable part of a process forward. I think this resonated with me because I have never really felt that I had anything like faith or hope, and I have just been sitting with that—put it that way.

It depends on the kind of faith though really, doesn't it? You get the faith of people who say they belong to a church and say God will look after this and that; they are quite certain that they need do nothing at all. There's the faith that Omar Khayyám speaks of, the 'blind faith, understanding replied'. I agree with you. I have never been able to have faith in the sense that you see everything's going to be all right. It's a faith which really believes in something practically impossible but knows that you have got to do something about it.

S. I think that is very much what I thought or felt. It's like having a belief that there is a way out of an impossible situation, and I think it came home to me that I had never really believed there was a way.

As I have said so often, you have to be an optimist, which means you have a right to have hope because one has a right not to be negative. If you can understand really that 90 per cent of all the occupation of our I's is negative, and you can see that if you can do away with that, then your whole situation is transformed immediately because the energies are different.

S. I have had days when I have tried to make an aim simply not to say anything negative—it was totally beyond me.

But one really has to understand that that is the situation. If one can understand that really right inside, then you are in a situation when you can begin not to be like that. But it can't be hoped that will change without doing something about it. There can't be just the faith that Allah will provide or God will do this or that without actually doing something. You know the saying—'Have faith in Allah, but first tie up your camel'. It has to be like that.

G. I think I need some optimism, because over the summer I have been having moments of fear that I am not working—that it is an illusion, that I am deluding myself, and I find I can feel very positive about a Work idea or a Work concept. But then when I come to actually do something about it I might try but then I lose sight of it and a lot of the time it seems to be hidden anyway. I find this particularly with the concept of lying, I find that incredibly difficult. Sometimes I can catch myself, but mostly I can't.

What you say is quite right. It is very hard actually, really to believe that there is a way out anyway, or that I can do it, or whether it should be me—why me especially? But this only comes if we really get a completely different view of the situation as it is, of my own particular situation. You see what could happen, if one could really understand that lying destroys all our possibilities. It actually is the one continuous occupation which destroys the real possibility we have. If I can understand that and let that really eat into me, then I have got a reason to stop lying. It can't be an academic reason like 'It's a good thing not to lie'. It has to be something that really is in your blood.

H. In the summertime I had a difficult holiday. I realise that my memory of this kind of struggle went back to J. not being there and fixing everything up and I realise that there is an enormous area which I never move into and it is associated with a fear. I was only able to see the edges of that. I could not get to the core of it, but one day I sat quietly in the morning and I said to myself 'This is life, welcome it'. I just saw that it tied in with the reading last time about adding to this kind of difficulty, a kind of imagined difficulty. It was something to do with the body. It was too hot—I was in a council flat, I didn't want to be there, there was no cooling system, people stayed up all night. It was all to do with the body and yet I felt that something turned and the holiday continued to be so-called 'difficult' like that. Even when I went to the most expensive hotel it was kind of the same. I saw the difficulty was myself making that and not opening up. I just feel I have got a tiny edge of something and I don't know if you can help me in any way to see this fear because I think it is probably a very big prison.

The amount of life one lives is not the number of days, weeks, months, it is the amount of experience we have. We are told we are born with something called essence. One can assume that on that essence is a pattern which is our own particular pattern, our own particular duty to fulfil in life. It can happen that we go through life completely unconsciously and it dies exactly the way it was born. In other words we have had practically no life even though we may have lived to 105. This really relates to death. We tend to think of death as something at the end of our particular life. Death is a continual process, it is all around us all the time. If I have a thought it lives and dies. An emotion lives and dies. A fly lives and dies. An elephant lives and dies. Every time anything dies it releases energy. This is the whole purpose of it. This is the Third Octave. A tiny little bit of energy is released from, say, a thought, and when you think of all the millions of people, all day long, pouring out these tiny bits of energy all of it goes to feed what Nature requires. That is dying unconsciously.

To die consciously is a completely different thing. This is Work. This is our possibility. You can come to the point where the negative side of me, the personality side of me, they finally die. But that energy, the energy of something dying consciously, is absorbed by itself. A phrase of Gurdjieff's which I never understood when I first heard it—'The results of a cause re-enter the cause'. Now if I can die with awareness, if I can die in that way, all that energy can go to the inner part of myself. I can keep that energy. This again is part of our possibility. This is the kind of thing I have to explore with my mind to try and understand this situation. This is the only way I will ever move. I can't tell you a particular formula to answer the question you asked me. What I can say is try and understand this. This is what will help you. This is what will help you with your lying. In other words we have now got to start growing up. We have got to think in a completely different way. To be able to think in such a way you find something inside that gives you a feeling inside as you take in impressions, with the way you are thinking. So you think all the time. Now realise that you are in the midst of death. It is going on all the time unconsciously and you have the possibility of dying each moment consciously.

D. Over the summer I was continuing to try and look very objectively at my outside life and trying to accept it, but I could see that a lot of the negativity came from, especially when dealing with other adults rather than children, having too great an expectation of other people. From that I haven't necessarily stopped it all, but I am very much more aware when I am making those kind of comments and have mainly tried to be more self-reliant and not have unrealistic expectations.

Try and turn it into experience. You can see a life going on with everything impinging on it and not realising it is happening, whereas a life where you actually realise what is happening to you and which you experience is a completely different kind of life.

S. You asked us to look at what we have gained from the last few months. It has been quite clear to me that I can see the need for working constantly. I see it differently, I don't know how. What you have just said I think has answered my question. It seems absolutely vital to me that I have to work. I feel it very strongly but then like G. says the reality is that one loses it very quickly. I felt that one of the things that touched me quite strongly recently was when we were doing that exercise on lying. I could see how the second I see something I lie about it to myself. What you said about experience means something as well. I made this sort of pact with myself that if I felt I was awake or I saw something then I would just not say anything or not think anything and just try and let it be there. I think that is what you mean by experiencing it. I am trying not to think negatively about it but I know I don't think enough. I know I have an experience, I don't take it further, I don't try and wrestle with it and I am trying to look at that now and see why I don't and see what it is that just goes 'Oh yes'.

You see something is happening—it doesn't matter what it is, maybe pleasant or unpleasant but *I am here.* I see it happening, I am here experiencing it. I am not trying to pretend it hasn't happened. I am not lying about it, getting resentful about it, I am here, it is happening. Any aspect of life you can treat like that, instead of which our normal method of resentment, or pushing it off, is really an unconscious act. We are just not believing it is there, and do anything we possibly can not to believe it is there. You see if you're dealing with somebody who normally you find difficult or you consider inwardly about them so much, you can see that there is a particular process going on there, which is cutting you off completely from life and from anybody else. If you can just change that you will find that all your relationships change immediately too. Then you have got to remember to allow your previous role to change. If you have a particular role with somebody which is different you have then got to change that role, let it go, or otherwise you will just fill that role and the same process will happen.

J. I found the break period quite difficult from the point of view of not having the interruption to my normal activity that being at a meeting or being at a Workday brings, and I could tell that just by merely associating with G. and T. although we never talked about the Work whilst there were other people around, it kept occurring to me that I had a connection with these people. And that was enough of an interruption to virtually alter my step. I feel quite hung up with this idea of lying. You said something earlier about bringing one's mind to bear and I realise I am hung up just because I don't really want to take it on board. I felt that maybe something to do with my education was part of that as well. One is brought up to tell the truth and all this sort of thing and I felt that I left all that behind; it is a bit of a dark shadow. It is also like somebody said about not being negative. If I actually reflect upon the last six weeks all I can taste and all I can hear is the sound of my voice being negative in certain situations. Sleep is sickeningly comfortable and I will only do something if I am forced by circumstance and one is always looking for success. Now that is all part of that lying for me. For instance I would be a bit depressed because I haven't received some money from someone. The minute the money comes, I am all up in the air–great. That makes me feel sick once that happens because of something watching it and from everything that has been said earlier this evening, I can see this is great material for me. I can just feel myself going fast asleep sometimes in associative situations and my dream is to see myself nice and busy, busy remembering myself. There was a term once used–internal dialogue–in the Castaneda book and this idea of withdrawing from that internal dialogue. I am just very aware of the radio, nice and loud in my head most of the time.

But you can't really retire from it. You have to put something else in its place.

J. I was going to say–if you don't lie what do you do then? But that sounds such a naïve question.

What really would make us work 24 hours a day? Fear?

J. Fear of death.

This is why you have got to think quite differently about your situation. See your particular life, see that it is a life among millions and millions of lives and you are constrained to follow the same pattern as everybody else but you don't have to. We have this possibility of fulfilling a real pattern which is given us to begin with provided we live consciously rather than just completely mechanically. Try and remember one parable in the New Testament about the seeds sown—when they fall on stony ground the birds come and pick them up, you can see negative thoughts stopping you being there. Some fall on ground where thistles form around them—very successful lives, very busy lives, so completely taken in by what is around them.

It is quite right to try and find moments to be quiet, put aside moments to be quiet, but eventually you have to really see that being quiet is not just a particular occupation at a given time it is something that has to happen all the time. You can in fact live in the midst of a very busy life without actually belonging to it. 'The lilies of the field, they toil not neither do they spin, yet Solomon in all his glory was not clothed as one of these'. All this attention that we pay to this or that, we don't have to. I can give all my attention to what I am doing quite properly in life, I can work hard but I still don't have really to belong to it. I can still be quiet inside. I can still realise that inside there is something I have to attend to. You are putting a screw into the wall. You put a screwdriver onto it. You realise a bit of attention is required to get it there and then you see that this is attention, attention I must have anyway but now consciously. You can really begin to live like this so that you experience all that you are doing—experience life. You see you have this possibility with the things you do regularly which go into your moving centre; you can in fact then have attention free to really look at what you are doing, experience what you are doing, something you do every day. Instead of doing the same thing unconsciously, you do it consciously. But you find in some strange way that what you do then becomes better, different.

Meeting 5

T. During the early part of this year I tried praying to another level–to show me my situation. But I could see nothing. More recently I felt like coming here and saying to you that I just can't do this work. I felt like chucking it in because it's a waste of time for me. But a few days ago I was transcribing some notes and you were saying something to G. about self, and suddenly it just tipped the balance–I could just see, or get a glimpse of, an understanding of self, how it belongs to life. How it has taken me from the cradle and it will take me to the grave. How it lives for itself.

A lot of things said in various kinds of groups completely overlook that. They talk about achieving enlightenment, the spirit or the soul in the abstract, but you cannot deny the fact that you live in life, that you belong to life. What has to be done has to be done alongside this. I was driving back from Loughborough today and while I was driving I was thinking about prayer. And that one cannot directly demand, or do something about the part with which you live life. It has to be something quite separate. But at the same time you must not try to deny it.

So the prayer I suggest you try, this method goes for everybody, you put your attention into your head. You know what a brain looks like, you've seen it in illustrations. So you are above your head and you're looking at your brain. You know that it is a part of you and its functions, to a very great extent, rule what you do and how you do it. And you will get a sensation there if you can put your attention deeply into it. You know that is part of you—part of your body. You can put attention into your breast which you can visualise as heart activity if you like. This is really where your heart is—you can visualise the physical heart. You know what a heart looks like, you've seen illustrations of it also, you actually look, feel, visualise your heart. And then you have sensation in this area. You know that your body works by itself miraculously, and at a speed beyond your calculation. You can visualise your body, you can sense your body, your limbs, your spine, and you are within the whole atmosphere of your body. So you can put your attention into your head, into your heart, into your body. Being aware of your breathing you put your attention into your head and say 'I'. You put your attention into your heart and 'feel'. Feel a tremendous desire—*wish*. You put your attention into your body and visualise what it would be '*to be*'.

Now you've gone into three separate parts. Now, putting your attention into your head and into your heart, you bring them together and say '*I wish*'. Those two together and say '*to be*'. Now you put your attention into your head, into your heart, into your whole body, you are now '*one*'. You have the strength in your mind, the desire of your feelings, and the place in your body and then say '*I wish to be*'. You see the difference there is, you are actually creating a place for something in which to live. You are not reaching out and saying 'I want'. Do you understand the difference? Well, that's a prayer. And if you do that, it creates something in the midst of life. You know that but for life you wouldn't be here. So you don't deny it, you create something additional within it.

C. Over the break I've been seeing more clearly what I've been talking about in the last few meetings. And I think I had an experience of accepting the way I am. I could see that I've always been the way I am from when I was very young. And I've visualised experiences in the past, and experienced emotions and the feelings that I had then. Experienced them very strongly, actually feeling them. And I see the power this has over me, that it rules my life completely. And as T. was saying, I can see that this is the way I was, this is the way I am, and I suppose how I will continue to be. But somehow there was something in me that could, for a moment, accept that this is the way I am. And at the same time for a moment there was a possible freedom from that. And I remember you saying to me a few months ago about starting from rock bottom, the only way from there is forward.

A couple of days ago I was walking on some downs; it was a nice day, an aeroplane flew overhead and I immediately thought of the last World War, what it must have been like for someone who had lost everything and had to start again from new. Somehow for a moment I could apply that to myself, to my situation. And again I had the feelings that I hadn't felt for years really. That everything around me was just beautiful, but not in a sentimental way, just the possibility of living differently.

It's remarkable isn't it, how these prison bars that seem so hard and strong, really can just melt away; because we do have that possibility.

C. You did say something else to me, I think in the last meeting, when I talked about my perpetual anxiety and you said that it was possibly something I had learned in the past, in my childhood, a way I found of existing. Could you say more about that please?

It's not for me to conjecture. I can have, perhaps, a very clear feeling about it but I think it's better for you to try and find it, particularly now. You can see that it is possibly something you can arrive at by your understanding of the way things are happening to you. On the other hand you can also see it's something you can just drop, it really doesn't matter. And that one of the most marvellous of all freedoms is to have no possessions of any kind whatsoever. So perhaps you can just leave it behind. But don't search for it. Allow yourself to look back at particular times, not anxiously but objectively.

L. When one is very quiet, in such a way as you have been talking about earlier with prayer, what is it that one must pick up to deal with life? At those times there is nothing but the prayer, but as you say you can't deny outer life. I've seen when I'm very quiet the part that comes back, as I watch it come back, is very flimsy. Is this just a mechanism for dealing with events? With what should one deal with life?

There's life as it is, as we exist within it, like fish in water, we live in that way. But there is also one's own life, which is a something within that life, like the millions of other lives like that. So you've only got to look at two things haven't you? See what it is you're really asking me, is it my own particular life that I can see or is it outer life generally? Outer life generally is far too great, far too powerful for us to even consider manipulating. We can see that it has a purpose of its own, which of course is beautiful as C. says. It's a legitimate thing, a process, and it doesn't particularly encourage us or even need us to do anything other than just live out our life from beginning to end. We have to be aware and understand that we have our own particular life which may, in fact, be a product of many times before, and memories of those times before. So the way we can see what I was really trying to tell T. is that there's no question of trying to demand or ferret out or struggle, it's a matter of really preparing a place or an area clean enough for our actual understanding of our situation. To '*be there*'. See that when we're quiet we move away from what we're normally involved with in our particular life. And for a moment we've moved away and we're saying really that that's there, I'm now cultivating something else. This is all we do; what knowledge exists is given to us eventually, into this part through our own particular growth of an area, an empty space if you like. And an area which is clean enough to receive the knowledge which, in fact, we know already.

L. *There's just two things that happened that made me ask this. One was some time ago when I was standing on a beach looking at the sea, it was quite wild and I tried to be aware of myself, and a strange sensation occurred where the sea, the waves and the wind just went straight through me. I found that made me uneasy as though I expected there to be something solid in myself. But there was nothing, there was just a hollow except for the part that was watching, seeing it happening. And then today in yoga we were given a relaxation exercise and there was this falling away of everything. Then already I was watching for the thing which would get up and start to move around and be back in interaction. What you said is helpful because perhaps what I'm asking about is our own purpose in life and because certainly I would have liked to have stayed in the place that was quiet. The part that had to get on and deal with life I did not want to be in.*

Years ago you were worried about having nothing inside. You must realise that you can only put something into something where there is a space for it. It's essential for that space to be there before you can fill it with something other than what it is already filled with—*activity.*

Workday

Morning

You will, certainly by now, accept the fact that we lie all the time and on every possible occasion we try and falsify the situation as it has happened. Looking at this with only the slightest objectivity it's really hard to see what advantage there is in it because we don't necessarily lie to other people, we lie to ourselves. It would seem to be just an occupation of a particular part of ourselves and it's an occupation which cuts us off from any possibility of seeing the reality of the situation.

After a certain amount of time working on oneself one can begin to see that there is an inner life—there's the possibility of an increased inner life—and at times we can actually accept the fact that there is a duality. There's my inner life and my outer life. My outer life is really one of almost complete fantasy, my inner life is small, fragile and it would seem, intermittent. We lie to ourselves even over this. For some strange reason we seem to deny that we have this possibility and prefer to immerse ourselves in the fantasy life. If we can find this inner part of ourselves and realise, at times, the feeling that it gives, we can see that in times of so called stress, or panic, or complete involvement in outer life, this inner part of ourselves can be a bit like a sheet anchor thrown out just to keep us steady while the fantasies pass.

What I'm trying to say to you is this, try and find this duality, try and be aware of it. See that one's purpose now must be to feed, nurture, discover, this inner part of oneself and accept at the same time, accept one's outer life. Working here today one can practise this, but I suggest that from now on this is what you must try and do. Try and understand that this is an essential part of the way you must live.

Today can possibly bring its difficulties because of the weather and I don't doubt you will probably find a few more, but from 10.15 a.m., every 25 minutes, I want you to pause, not stop, pause and try and feel, understand what I've been saying about this duality. I must feed, care, for my inner life and accept all that goes with my outer life. I say pause, because it's essential, if you really are going to pursue this for the rest of your life, that you must be able to be in between these two. Your outer life will never stop for you, but you can separate from it, even in the midst of it.

Lunchtime

D. I can see I don't really accept my outside life. I've seen it that many times, and I still don't want to face it, I run away from it.

What do you mean by accept? You don't like it?

D. I both do and don't in a way, I complain to myself about it, that sort of thing, rather than just accepting it.

You complain about the nature of it? You see to accept it really means you accept it as it is and all that belongs to it, just as it is. Then you can see that if you do that, there is no more negativity, no more arguing with it; you just accept it. What you would normally find coming at you, you just don't accept it. Strangely, you see, that's what happens.

D. I can see that is the thing to do, but I'm incapable of doing it.

Of course you are. Nobody said you were capable, but you've got to see this. Maybe you do this and suddenly accept for a moment or so and just gradually change. You can't accept your outside life completely until your inner life is strong enough, large enough, because you've nothing to accept it with.

J. I found the idea of accepting one's outer life to be a very attractive idea, for one reason because if one accepted one's outside life, this process of lying would be pretty much curtailed I imagine. Like you've just said, I did wonder what it is that accepts your life, because like everybody else I'm happy to accept my life when I think it is going along swimmingly, so it is just this sort of exchange between I's generally that I accept in my outside life. On a Workday like today there's a taste of accepting the fact that you've got very little control over your outside life.

I thought I had a slight clue to the idea of accepting my life; I said I want to work to my real possibilities. Yet I don't think I know what they are, and I am always conditioning, 'Oh I can't do that', or, 'We can't do that'.

The strange situation is that we actually run ourselves down when we don't accept that part of us. Nobody said one can. One can, but not in the way we normally think. You see, if you take away all the attitudes and opinions and all that, one is then open to accept things in a completely different kind of way, without any activity. We still have these feelings about our life, whether it's good or bad, or what makes it good or bad. It is just a very small part of the part which is life, the part of us, which actually belongs to the Third Octave. And if one thinks about it, you can think it is terrible sometimes, but the following day it is quite different, isn't it? The disaster, which was going to strike, never does. It's all part of the fantasia in which we live. So what we have to accept is that situation. Try and understand it. What we have to accept is complete fiction really.

K. *It's the acceptance without activity that I find so hard. If I can see parts of myself that are making my life difficult, I can begin to accept, but then I find it hard not to try to change it, I want to do something about it.*

As you were really saying there, the part of our life that we don't like is really our own creation. It isn't actually life itself; it's the reaction to it. So, if I can accept it, if I can, by this acceptance, increase the other side of myself, then that's the only way that life can change, because I then attract a different kind of situation. You see at any given moment, *I attract the life I am living.*

K. *So one should welcome the disasters as opportunities?*

They are not disasters, you just look at them, just accept them. You don't say, 'I don't want them'. You don't say, 'I wish this were different'. And you don't welcome the nice bits either; you just see them and accept them.

To go back to this duality, you have to see that they are really closely related. What happens in one's inner life is closely related to the way one accepts one's outer life.

L. I didn't think of my outer life in terms of the good things and the bad things or what I had to accept about it in that way. I felt it in terms of everything, I think. In everything that I was drinking in at any given moment, that was my outer life. So I felt, often, what is my inner life in relation to that?As you said the inner life is very small. If I pause or stop for a minute do I find my inner life then? Often I'm just finding more of my outer life. So I didn't have quite such a clear separation.

You can't really look for your inner life, you just have to understand that one has to cultivate the idea by going there, by putting one's attention there and away from the outer life.

You see you've got to really be between the two, it's not a matter of separating from it, it's actually being aware that there are two. Not until you can be aware of this over and over again does that inner life begin to grow.

S. I noticed that when I'd been quiet, I felt that the quality of that was what I wanted to bring to my outer life, in as much as that, for a second, you are just actually there where you are, rather than somewhere else.

Yes. You don't want to '*do*' anything. It manifests by itself. You see, you must not have this activity. You must not try to partake and do things.

S. Just look at it.

Yes. If I'm aware of my inner life, then what I'm doing outside will of itself be different. But if I start trying to make things happen then I'm not, I'm going there where I shouldn't be, involved in my normal business of fiddling with things and trying to manipulate.

S. Your energy is in your outer life, in what you're doing?

The energy is in *you*. There's my outer life and there's my inner life. I'm not trying to be in either of them. I just see that I have to accept what is going on outside and I have to feed the inner life.

Try to actually understand that, when you are doing it. I know for years and years I have tried to explain to you that it is not what one thinks, but what one is, that makes one different.

K. I think it's an example of lying. I caught myself remembering three or four minutes late for a couple of 25 minute periods and doing this contradictory, 'Well that doesn't matter because I was remembering earlier', and then catching all this fabrication.

Incredible really, isn't it? And what does it serve, that's the thing. Try it again now and see how it goes. Try and see that I don't want activity. I'm not in the situation of trying to manipulate my outer life, I just see if I'm cutting grass that's my outer life for that moment, I just accept that. And the attitude with which I do that is what can feed my inner life.

Evening

N. I came today with the intention that when I was here I was really going to be here and work in the proper way, in the way one would wish to work. It related to a piece I'd read in 'In Search of the Miraculous'. Gurdjieff was talking about prayer and mentioned how to pray properly, and that if someone is just reciting words, even a thousand times, and thinking of when their dinner is going to be, it was self-deceit. Similarly, for me on a Workday, I will come and try to put my all in, but by the afternoon I'm really flagging and finding I am thinking about home and what's going to happen and what the time is. That started to creep in a little bit this afternoon, but I just kept coming back to myself and thinking, 'No, I'm here and I wish to be here till the time comes when I have to go', and funnily enough we had to stay longer anyway. So perhaps that could be trying to accept what life is offering me today.

Yes, going towards it. The thing really is, about accepting one's outer life, that one has another purpose in life, another role in life, another wish, another something else. You can see how it can be all outer life and nothing else, can't it? But if one has another purpose then things fall into perspective and that is feeding your inner life.

N. At lunchtime you spoke about attitude feeding one; I'd never thought of that before, this morning I was just thinking in terms of trying to take in impressions, but I sort of felt a slight understanding of what you said.

And it is that attitude that shows up tremendously when I see people working in movements. I see this attitude, whether it is, to varying degrees, showing their wish to work, or whether it's, to use an Arabic word we used in the army, just alaquifik. Which is untranslatable, but it means, as we thought, any old how!

J. Having a target to finish a job on a Workday, well as best I can, is for me a bit like a cage. The minute you step in, you're in and you're sort of stuck until you can get out, and the only way out is to finish. This cuts down an awful lot of dreaming for me and what it did today was to give me an opportunity, from time to time, when we paused, to just sense the kind of old J. who just likes to try and get through the thing. I felt quite unworried, quite unconnected to my particular physical effort, but almost quite young in that other aspect, asking, 'what is my inner life at this moment in this situation?' It was almost as if, in the hubbub of working, there were times and moments, when F. reminded us to stop, to ponder that and that stopping helped. It's not as if I pondered it mentally, one started to kind of sense a state.

Absolutely. It's really what 'ponder' means, that's how I understand it. It's not a mental activity.

J. Often, I find when people work together in the ordinary way, they are quite violent when they work closely together. They are very aware of personal space, that kind of nonsense. I was very aware, even just walking out into the yard, that somebody would walk past and they wouldn't have that kind of atmosphere trailing and yet they wouldn't have that kind of 'hi-de-hi happy holiday' feel either. It was very subtle, but very different.

S. With regard to what was said about attitude and also what you said about activity; I was in the garden this afternoon and I could just see that I wasn't there. I was feeling that I didn't want to be there. My back was hurting and I thought that this is ridiculous, I've got to do something. I came in and listened to the tape. I think it's probably the first time ever on a Workday that I've stopped working and I saw how ridiculous it was to be there, to be seen to be working, but not to be doing anything at all.

I listened to the tape and I found myself really trying to understand what was being said rather than just sort of listening to it. Then I went out into the garden and did a bit of trimming and I could see that I was just there, it was different. However, I have a feeling, I haven't exactly seen it, but to me it must be true, that every time I think I want to work or I have the urge to work, or I think I'm working, I put something onto it. I just feel that I'm never actually doing it.

It's lying, isn't it?

S. Yes. There's always that. Like J. was saying about pondering, the minute I think about what an exercise is or how it should be, there's something that just comes in and sits on top of it.

This is activity, do you see?

Well it's been an interesting day, hasn't it? Goodnight and thank you very much.

The Value of Exercises

The exercises I give you on a Workday are always difficult. When one is here on that day, within the surroundings here, you have a chance of trying something which is a little more difficult. As much as anything else, an exercise really shows you what you can't do. Because if I was to tell you that you can't do this or that, you can't hold onto to your attention for more than two or three minutes at the outside, you would not believe me. One's nature is like that. But if you can demonstrate it, experience it for yourself, it's the best chance.

That is certainly one aspect of exercises. In addition, one really has to learn what one cannot do without being negative about it. It's not a question of failure, it's a question of actually accepting the fact of what one's situation really, truly is. Then when you try that exercise in 10 or 15 years time, you will get something quite different from it.

Breathe. Be aware of your breathing.

What is called meditation is being as quiet as you possibly can be, and then dropping an idea in. You allow it to be there and you will be surprised, if you can do this, how you can really understand very much more. More than by the so-called process of thinking.

When you hold an idea or thought, you hold it so that you can divorce it from its associations. They all have associations. You divorce it from the associative part of oneself, hold it as it is, then just be quiet. Be aware of your breathing and allow it to mature.

When we speak of remembering ourselves, it is really another way of saying, 'I'm being conscious'. Of course we know that consciousness is a very difficult term to define and it is something we find in different degrees. There are times when we know we are very much more aware, more conscious than at other times.

You know from observations of yourself that to a great extent one is passive and this is an attitude which is forced upon you by the nature of things. To avoid being passive one has to make some inner effort. So try today to remember yourself through the attitude one has towards the day.

I've come here voluntarily; I've come here because I feel I can get some benefit. Therefore, I must all the time try to have that positive attitude, try to let it flow.

Instead of making particular efforts, try to get the whole feeling.

Remember too, as I have said before, when I really, truly remember myself, it is the energy of my head, the energy of my feelings and the energy of my body blended together. So I try to put my attention into my head, my body and my feelings simultaneously and allow that energy—*allow,* that's really the word I'm looking for—you allow yourself to be given to this attitude which you want to hold. 'Casting bread upon the waters,' it comes back.

There's no hard effort, just a constant inner pressure on the attitude, on the attitude which I want to have. Just allow it to be, remind yourself what you can gain, what you've come here for.

I can, you see, remember my head, I can remember my body, I can remember my feelings, but behind that there is some wish. If I can be aware of all that I get the benefit of the energies of my head, my body and my feelings to help me remember myself. To get the full benefit from this kind of attitude I must not, of course, be in any way tense or negative. It can be the kind of day when one can be very happy and grateful.

To be aware of the beauty of the perfume of roses is the right function for your emotions. When you work with your body you get some really good feelings sometimes. When you use it properly, getting exercise with everything flowing is the right feeling from the right use of your body. What about your head? There is a right use for it, one can really apply one's thought if one wishes.

We mention being aware of each centre; however, you can make the mistake of being stuck in that centre too closely instead of just being there and moving away from it. You see this totality of yourself. Look at it differently. There's the energy going out of your head, out of your feelings, out of your body. Be aware of that and be aware of your breathing, be aware of a breath, two or three breaths, very deeply at the same time.

I know I've got my head, I know I've got my feelings and my body. I've observed this so many times. I just have to have that knowledge, that awareness there. Be aware of energy that is going out. And then bring in my attention. And what I am then doing is taking it away from those centres, and then I gather it all together and I am aware of my breathing, the breath, the air, I feel the air going through the nostrils, the back of the throat into the lungs.

You'll see there's a tremendous something that takes place when that air hits the lungs, meets the blood. That happens all the time and we don't even know it. Know it, try to experience it, at the same time as keeping all the other within your experience.

It isn't easy, but it's terribly important to get this taste of what it would be for a moment to be just a different thing, a different being, functioning quite differently.

Then, as it is said, '*Life is real only then, when I am*'.

To Prepare

Try to set aside some time during the day, preferably in the morning. Try to sit in a position which is not normal, not like you are sitting now. You'll see that there is a limited repertoire of feeling and thoughts and they are all connected with a particular position or stance. And if I have that thought or feeling it tends to bring that position, or if I fall into that position it brings that thought. So I try to sit in a way in which I don't ordinarily sit and in which I have to maintain my attention to stay in that position.

If you can sit in a Lotus position, crossed legs, absolutely comfortably, very good, do that. Otherwise, sit like this with your back straight, head upright, legs together, hands resting in your lap. Eyes open or closed.

Practice using attention. Without it we can't really do anything. We don't know what it is, but it is made of some very fine energy. All the time it is being taken out of us by the way the attention fastens on this or that thought or feeling. This we refer to as being identified. Being identified with something.

When you sit quietly, practice putting your attention into your hand. Hold it there as long as you can, try to get sensation in depth with attention. Gradually you'll be able to move this all over your body. This is very important.

Being Quiet

Try to make the effort to see that you're going to have all this activity and you *will* lose yourself and you cannot possibly expect otherwise. But try to get quiet just for a moment or so and visualise taking that with you throughout the day. Carrying it inside even though all the activity is going on do you see? See that you are going to be asleep, it's the condition in which we live. But to be aware of the sleep while you're in it is something quite different. If you think about that it is a miracle by comparison with just being asleep isn't it?

Sometimes when you sit in the mornings, relaxing, being quiet, it's more successful than other days isn't it? Other days it just doesn't seem possible. That's how it is.

There's a very interesting process that takes place when one comes to the realisation that one has to do something about oneself. We start doing our best to observe ourselves and the first thing we discover of course is not our reality, we discover our abnormality, our dreams, our tensions and so to begin with we're in a worse situation than we were in before because we find it hard to relax. We are feeling our tensions, we are seeing them and forgetting the fact that previously we thought we were relaxed and were just not aware it. So it is a great problem that most people go through when they start looking at themselves, trying to relax, trying to remember themselves. They are just faced with so many difficulties and tensions, visions of what was not visible before.

There is the relaxation of this body but also an inner relaxation. You'll find that this body can relax on many different levels, in many different energies. You can relax in your head and you can be tense in your emotions. Look at relaxation and see what it means to be relaxed inside when you are in the depths of really trying to do this exercise. You will find it will move you away from lots of the tension in which you are normally caught.

When we really see our situation, we see we are constant movement, constant turbulence, carrying around an enormous number of attitudes and opinions. There is so much noise going on. So occasionally, if that quietens down, we just see things quite differently. This is what I call getting near to being normal. Really, how do I want to live?

I feel that the Work has given me the possibility to take responsibility for my life and the things that happen in my life.

I see that I have the opportunity to give less and less value to the fear and guilt that I have carried with me all my life, and with this comes the understanding that I know so little and am so little.

Rather than feeling diminished, this gives me the greater freedom and strength to live my life. The opportunities are endless if only I can clear the fog and see them. Laziness and imagination are the stumbling blocks.

Being Objective

It's stressed very often, that our observation, self-observation, should be objective. When we use words continuously we tend to forget why we are actually doing this, what is the purpose of being objective?

Being objective is very, very difficult.

As we know, from experience we have lots of little I's in us which are not really interested in what we want to do. If we persist in trying to be objective, we can eventually encourage some of those I's to come together. We can then form another 'I', perhaps what you might call an *'observing I'*.

This also is a foundation, an addition, a strengthening of, what is referred to as our magnetic centre. In other words we are building up something which is quite separate and more conscious than the amorphous mass of little I's.

So that's the reason for being objective.

Now frequently we know when we try to be present, we make an effort, and there's a different feeling, we see things differently just for a moment. If I go further, and if I make the effort to be present and also make the effort to be able to say *'I am'* then I am again being objective.

We know from experience this doesn't last long, a matter of seconds, perhaps minutes if possible. When I am in that state then I have an objective part inside of me which is also strengthening this observing 'I', this growing 'I' inside me.

It comes back again to what I have said so many times, that we have to pretend. In other words, my efforts to be objective, my efforts to be *'I am'* while I am feeling present, are all strengthening and encouraging the growth of something quite separate inside.

So we try to remember that to be objective, that to be present plus the effort to be able to feel and say '*I am*', is work towards growing, developing a separate part of myself which is the beginning of being real. If you think about this, you see that this kind of effort is not for an immediate result. It is to do something which is not necessarily immediately obvious. As we say so often, this Work is parabolic.

So today really make the effort to be present and then say '*I am*'.

We come back to it, fail, come back, fail and we come back. What if we fail? It doesn't matter! It's the effort of doing it. Let's be quiet for a moment and consider what we are going to do.

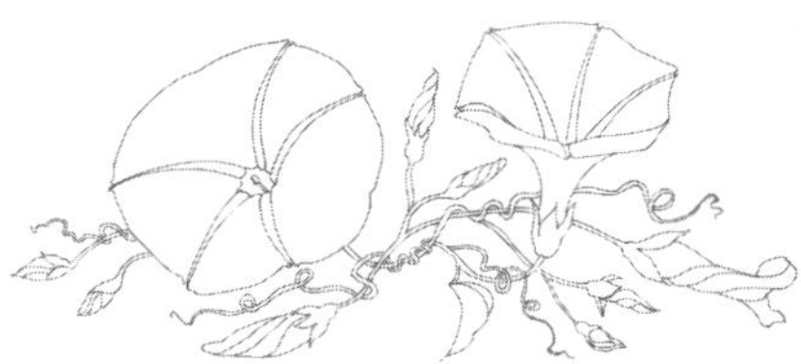

Some of my family have been involved in the Work for many years. It was not until I had left London, Norfolk and England and went to live in France that the necessity of joining the group 'opened' itself up to me. Suddenly there was a sense of urgency, of survival; that everything I had heard from my family about the Work seemed obvious and so necessary.

The contact with the group in Norfolk is infrequent but nevertheless valuable as the Work becomes harder and more demanding.

I feel change coming about but in a totally different way; something solid being created slowly, held there by struggling and not letting go.

Deep Thought

We were talking the other day about the Commanding Self which really is the sum total of everything we can find in ourselves that completely runs our life.

This kind of conjecture can be completely academic and can be something that we just think about, and can go on for years and years. But if we are to find out anything real it doesn't happen accidentally. That part of us is conscious, and living as we do, everything we do is utterly mechanical and conscious things cannot happen accidentally.

What I am really suggesting is that there is a justification for applying one's curiosity, applying one's mind, one's wish to know something. So if one takes the idea (*a*) that there is great deal which is mechanical and (*b*) that there's a possibility of another part being conscious, then that is something about which one can think quite deeply. I suggest you do that today. Whatever else you do keep coming back to this as an idea.

You see if I or someone else tells you that there is an *A* and there is a *B* and you believe it, that doesn't get you anywhere. If you can, by conscious application, real thought, experience this, that is what counts. And as some of you probably know the response or reward from this kind of effort doesn't necessarily come immediately. It can come years later, but it can't come unless one has exercised oneself in that direction.

Gurdjieff used the phrase, 'working like a man'. By this he meant working in a completely balanced way. You know how very often you get a glimpse of yourself, find yourself totally ruled by your head or your feelings. Your body just driven. If you can see, visualise, the 'I' of the head just completely immersed in itself, the 'I' of one's emotions just self-consumed, you can then get the experience sometimes of the 'I' moving out of there, and looking at the head, or seeing the feelings. If one could visualise the I's of the head, the feelings and the body withdrawing and looking at the head, the feelings and the body, then they would become one.

The head, feelings and body would then be working under obligation, with, so to speak, a spectator. This would be a balanced way of working.

So today, as you work, try to keep coming back, observing as often as you possibly can, and try to get a spectator of all three selfs. If you can do this you'll find that one is dominating. Only under objective observation do we separate from that one self. Try to imagine, visualise, drawing out an 'I' from each self and making it into one observing 'I'.

Do this as often as you can, then say to yourself, '*I am*'.

To give meaning to that one really needs a certain emotional content, a kind of emotional energy that belongs to wish as distinct from the ordinary emotion that consumes us and with which we identify.

So when you say, '*I am*', you feel '*I wish to be*'.

Breath

You see to have attention in one breath demands quite a lot, and to maintain it for another breath this attention must be retained; it must be really one breath, pause out, pause in, pause, with my attention all the time, successive attention so to speak. Is that clear?

Do it at least once a day if you can, but you won't do it right away. This is a very big effort but it is something which can change you, it can give you a completely different idea of what the Work is. It can change the physical and the psychic material inside you. Then, do not alter your way of breathing. It must be relaxed. Avoid tension.

M. When I try to do that, to concentrate on my breath, I can see that it only lasts the one breath.

The fact that I am breathing is not the same thing as awareness of one's own breath. To be aware of the very texture of it and what it does as it comes in, what it does in the lungs, you have to have your attention there. You have to have your attention in so many places in this, the air is a food and you can get to feel it feeding in a physical way. At the same time with your attention there your impressions are also creating energy which goes to feed the other part of yourself which desperately needs food. Nowadays there's a common idea of breathing, like yoga breathing, that one is aware of breathing. This is fine, it normally doesn't do you any harm and it feeds your body. But what I am talking about now is something quite different.

So try looking at this overall; as I was saying, I am aware of my breath, its nature and the function of breathing. I have unbroken attention for at least three breaths, it is as if three breaths were one with no break whatever in my attention. I become aware of my physical body, I become aware of something else and I say '*I am here now*'. I can be aware of the impressions coming in, there will be a sensation there creating, transforming the energy to a finer energy. You see there is a lot there. If you were a Zen monk sitting there and you lost a fraction of that you would be hit by the Master. You have to be your own Master.

It's very often useful to try breathing like this. Breathe in and know you are taking in energy, you're feeding. You hold it and you breathe out and know you are passing out your negativity, poisons or whatever you want to lose. Three breaths like that can very often open up something for you, but you have got to do it with as much attention as you possibly can, attention, sensation, understanding, visualisation, everything all at once as it comes in. It changes your bloodstream, it makes a tremendous difference in the Food Octave, and then psychologically you can use that breath to take out and get rid of what you want to lose.

If you observe closely you will see that every breath has a different thought, just idle thoughts. You are subject to this from life. I've told you before that as far as Nature is concerned we are just cows, it's part of the process. If '*I am*', I can see that every breath can bring a different thought, which is why if you can manage to hold your attention without thought for three breaths you've created an enormous amount of energy and space. Before one starts this process, one has to make oneself present otherwise one is just trying to inject something into the ordinary stream of repetitive, associative thought.

Epilogue

When new people come to see if they can join the group and I ask them what they want to do with their life they frequently say, that above all, they wish to help other people. This of course, is very laudable, but to help people it is necessary to have the means, to want is not enough. One can really only help others in the measure that one can help oneself.

Also, can one see what help others really need? There is a little story I like which highlights this.

There was this cat sitting by the edge of the wood. 'Look', he said, 'at all those rabbits over there. Here am I willing to give them half price lessons on how to catch mice and not one of them is interested'.

So often we see that the help which is offered to others is of the nature of making rabbits eat mice.

I am sometimes asked what is the end result of the Work; to me, it is to become a real individual, with inner freedom, with one's own morality, who can help and serve others.